THE PUBLIC
SPEAKER'S
JOKE BOOK

Also available from Elliot Right Way Books

Quick Quips & Longer Jokes*
The Right Joke For The Right Occasion*
Wedding Speeches
Sample Social Speeches
Your Voice: How To Enrich It, And Develop It For Speaking,
   Acting And Everyday Conversation

* By the same author

THE PUBLIC SPEAKER'S JOKE BOOK

Kevin Goldstein-Jackson

RIGHT WAY

CONTENTS

DEDICATION

This book is dedicated to my two young daughters, Sing Yu (who kindly helped sort the jokes into alphabetical order) and Kimberley.

The Public Speaker's Joke Book is also dedicated to all my friends and acquaintances who kindly made suggestions for it; and to my wife, Mei Leng, in the hope that she will prefer this book to my cheque book!

INTRODUCTION

My last joke book had astronomical sales (three astronomers bought a copy of it) so the publishers asked me to write *The Public Speaker's Joke Book*.

This book contains 1039 jokes, which have been listed alphabetically under various subject headings, although sometimes it has been very difficult to decide under which of a number of equally appropriate headings a joke should appear.

There is also a Directory section to assist in finding the most appropriate joke for the occasion.

The term 'public speaker' has been used in its widest sense: anyone who at any time has to speak in public – not only people speaking at parties, dinners, receptions, conventions – but even the much more difficult task of filling in time at a children's party when the magician has got lost and will be arriving late (just let the children laugh and groan by using the jokes in the Questions and Knock, Knock sections).

The jokes range from the old to the new, from the bold to the slightly blue, and from groan-making to side-splitting.

In the interests of equality there are sections of jokes about Boyfriends and Husbands.

Hopefully, there is something in this book suitable for every public speaker. But try to choose the right joke for the right audience. A sick joke should not be brought up in polite conversation.

Some of the jokes mention certain towns (like Basingstoke and Bournemouth) but most of these can easily be changed to the place where the public speaker is speaking or to a similarly appropriate town or city.

If you are nervous about making a speech, start with a modest apology – like: 'Before I begin my speech I'd like to warn you that I'm suffering from a severe handicap – I'm sober.'

Remember that a bore is a person with nothing to say who insists on saying it. The best speeches are like a well-kept lawn: short and neat.

If a joke 'falls flat' just ignore the reaction and continue, or say something like: 'That was a joke specially designed for people with a way out sense of humour – whenever I tell it, people look for the way out.'

If anyone should heckle, simply comment: 'Thank you for giving us a piece of your mind. It's a pity you don't have much left.' Or you could say: 'I hear you are going into hospital next week for a brain operation – the doctors hope to give you one.' Or 'The last time I saw something that looked like you I threw it a peanut.'

Finally, you may like to know that a psychologist has proved that jokes are healthy because laughter helps people to relax, and laughter and fun 'give your heart, lungs, face, shoulders and diaphragm a really good workout.'

I sincerely hope that some of the jokes in this book will help you to spread some health and happiness to your next audience.

Good luck – and best wishes.

KG-J

DIRECTORY

On this, and the following three pages is the Directory to the 1039 jokes in this book.

If you are *not* searching for a particular joke/subject and are just reading this book for fun (or there's nothing else to read in the toilet) then just skip all these pages and start on page 13.

The numbers given below refer to the number of the joke and *not* to the page number.

A

1. The company personnel department had carefully interviewed thirty-eight people for the job of assistant to the financial director.

The chief executive thought that one candidate – Charles – seemed ideal. Charles had been to a major public school. Not only was he a qualified accountant, but Charles also had a masters degree in business administration. He seemed fully aware of the latest creative accountancy techniques.

'Charles,' said the chief executive, 'we've decided to offer you the job. And as you're so well qualified we've decided to start you off on a slightly higher salary than the one advertised. We'll pay you £48,000 a year.'

'Thank you,' replied Charles. 'But how much is that per month?'

ACTORS

2. The Hollywood actress liked her tenth husband so much she decided to keep him for an extra fortnight.

3. The young actress was delighted to get a part with real meat in it. She had to dress up as a bun for a commercial for hamburgers.

4. I was once asked to play the part of a vampire's victim in a Hollywood movie, but I turned it down. I don't do bit parts.

5. The leading actress was most upset on her opening night. She only received seventeen bouquets of flowers. Yet she had paid the florist to send twenty.

AFFAIRS

6. A friend of mine has just spent ten thousand pounds on a little peace and quiet. His little piece wanted the ten thousand to keep it quiet from his wife.

7. The husband was furious. 'Is it true you've been having an affair with John?' he angrily asked his wife.

'Yes,' replied the wife.

'Then,' said the husband, 'I'm going round to his house and I'll teach him a lesson . . .'

'But darling,' said the wife, 'couldn't you take a few lessons from him instead and then I wouldn't need to have an affair?'

AGE

8. I wouldn't say my wife tells lies about her age – but does she really expect people to believe that she gave birth to our son at the age of three?

9. You know you're old when you recall that in your youth a kiss happened at the end of a beautiful evening. Today, a kiss means it's the start of a *fantastic* evening.

10. I think I've just reached the out-age. When you reach fifty everything seems to spread out, fall out or wear out!

AMBIDEXTROUS

11. He'd give his right arm to be ambidextrous.

B

BANKS

12. 'Why,' asked Mr White, 'are you still overdrawn at the bank?'

'I don't know,' replied his wife. 'They sent me a bank statement last month and a letter saying I was five hundred pounds overdrawn. Then they sent me another letter insisting I pay the five hundred pounds within seven days. So I paid it promptly. I immediately wrote them a cheque for the money.'

BARBER

13. Barber: 'Sir, how would you like your hair cut?'
Customer: 'Off.'

BARGAIN

14. A bargain is something you buy that is cheaper than something you really want or need.

BAT

15. The bat was very tired. It sunk lower and lower until it did not have enough energy to flap its wings any more and so it flopped to the ground.

After a few minutes it crawled along the grass until it came to the old trees where it lived. Then it suddenly raced towards the trees, stopped when it almost hit them, then went backwards.

Then it raced towards the trees again.

It did this so many times that I became curious.

'Why are you racing towards the trees, stopping, going backwards, then racing towards them again?' I asked.

The bat sighed, then said (for it was a talking bat): 'I was very run down and so I needed to charge my bat-trees!'

BEES

16. Why were there so many bees in the toilet at the petrol station?

Because they saw the sign advertising BP.

BIBLICAL

17. It's quite obvious that Adam, the first man in the world, was an idiot. There he was, in paradise with a beautiful, naked woman and what does he want to do? Kiss and cuddle? Make love? No – he wants to eat fruit!

18. Adam was the world's first book-keeper. He turned over a leaf and made an entry.

BIGAMY

19. The only thing that prevents me from being a bigamist is the thought of having two mothers-in-law.

BIRDS

20. The two birds met for the first time in a tree and one of them said: 'Bred any good rooks recently?'

BIRTH

21. When Claude's wife was expecting their second child he told his three-year-old son that soon a giant stork would be arriving and it would land on the chimney of their house. In the stork's beak would be a wonderful present.'

'Oh,' said Claude's son, 'I hope it will be quiet and won't upset mummy. A giant bird suddenly arriving like that might give her a shock. And that wouldn't be any good as you know you made her pregnant and she's expecting a baby.'

22. The new doctor was making his round of the maternity ward and the first five women he saw were all expecting their babies on the same day: 28th March.

The doctor moved on to look at the sixth patient.

'And when is your baby expected?' asked the doctor.

'I don't know,' replied the woman, 'I didn't go to the office party like the other women in here did.'

23. When my husband was born it wasn't a stork that delivered him – it was a vulture.

BIRTHDAYS

24. When I was a child my family were so poor that the only thing I got on my birthday was a year older.

25. My husband said he wanted a tie for his birthday that matched the colour of his eyes – but where can you find a bloodshot tie?

26. My wife refuses to use Inter Flora for people's birthdays. She says she doesn't think people would like margarine as a present.

27. It's my wife's birthday tomorrow. Last week I asked her what she wanted as a present.

'Oh, I don't know,' she said. 'Just give me something with diamonds.'

That's why I'm giving her a pack of playing cards.

BOOKS

28. *Is It In The Stars?* by Zoe D Ack.

29. *Great Eggspectations* by Charles Chickens.

30. *In The Soup* by Minnie Stroney.

31. *How Sherlock Holmes Quickly Solved Crimes* by L M N Tree.

32. *Big Celebrations* by Annie Versary.

33. What do you get if you throw a copy of *The Canterbury Tales* in the air?
  A flying Chaucer.

34. What was enormous, very heavy, lived a long time ago and liked *Wuthering Heights* and *Jane Eyre*?
  A Bronte-saurus.

35. My next book is about two families who constantly fight and argue – it's a work of friction!

36. My books of prose may be bad, but they could be verse.

37. I once knew an author who changed his name to biro because he wanted a pen name.

38. The world's shortest book contained no words. Its title was: *All I Know About Women*.

BORES

39. A bore is someone who opens his mouth and puts his own feats in it.

40. Bores are people who don't know that the best speeches are like a well-kept lawn: short and neat.

BOYFRIENDS

41. My boyfriend is a kung-fu expert. Last night he hit an insect on his side and broke one of his own ribs.

42. On my first date with my boyfriend I asked him if I could hold his hand, and he said: 'I can manage, thank you. It isn't very heavy.'

43. My boyfriend has a good head for money – it's got a little slot in the top . . .

44. I wouldn't say my boyfriend was stupid, but when we went to the park last night and I said I saw a poor, dead bird, he asked 'Where?' and looked up at the sky.

45. Most of my sister's boyfriends are like eggs – fresh, rotten or hard-boiled.

46. When my friend Albert discovered that his girlfriend was being unfaithful to him he asked her: 'Why do you need another lover? Have you had enough of me?'
   'Darling,' replied his girlfriend, 'it's because I *haven't* had enough of you that I need a lover.'

47. My boyfriend was told about the birds and bees very early in life. Shortly afterwards he was stung by a bee – and was extremely worried for the next nine months.

48. Somehow, I don't think I'm going to marry my current boyfriend. Last night when I casually asked him how much money he had in the bank he said he would have to go home and open the pig to find out.

BUS TRAVEL

49. The first time I went to Bournemouth I wanted to visit Compton Acres Gardens in Poole. I joined a bus queue, and as a bus approached I asked the elderly lady in front of me: 'Excuse me, does this bus go to Compton Acres?'

'Yes,' replied the lady, 'just get off the bus two stops before the stop I get off.'

BUSINESS PEOPLE

50. The tired, exhausted businessman had felt compelled to drink more than he could really cope with at a business lunch at which he had lost his firm's major client.

The businessman staggered back to the office and asked his gorgeous secretary: 'Can you give me something to ease my pain?'

'How about something tall and cold?' replied the secretary.

'Don't!' said the businessman. 'Don't bring my wife into it.'

51. When I asked my boss for a salary rise because I was doing the work of three men he said he couldn't increase my pay, but if I told him the names of the three men he'd fire them.

52. I'm always delighted when people stick their noses in my business – my company makes paper tissues.

53. My husband's business is rather up-and-down – he makes yo-yos.

54. When Bernard got fired from his last job they were really tough. They made him hand back his keys to the executive toilets, return his company credit card, give back his company car, and even give back his ulcer!

55. Last night I discovered why my boss hired *me* rather than all the other candidates to be his deputy. Over a lengthy business dinner he admitted that when he interviewed all the other candidates they seemed to be the cleverest, most dynamic people in the world.

Yet when he interviewed me, I managed to convince him that *he* was the cleverest, most dynamic person in the world.

56. Another friend of mine is a very successful businessman. He started with five thousand pounds – now he owes fifty-five million.

57. I once knew a man who was always travelling abroad for business meetings. One trip lasted two whole months and towards the end of it he could stand it no longer and went to the local brothel.

'I would like your most bored, tired, fat lady,' he said.

'Why do you want someone like that?' asked the surprised madam.

'Because,' replied the businessman, 'I've been away for so long I'm homesick for my wife!'

58. I once knew a couple who were in the iron and steel business – she did the ironing, while he went out stealing.

BUTCHER

59. The lady was searching for the last word in value in Christmas turkeys. The butcher showed her a bonny bird but she hesitated and asked if he had a slightly bigger one.

'I will have a look in the cold store,' said the butcher, and disappeared for a minute or two.

In fact it was his last bird so what he did was to ruffle all the feathers up and put the bird into a shallow box so that it would look bigger.

'Here we are,' he said, 'is this all right?'

'Ooh, now that *is* super,' said the woman. 'I think I will take both!'

C

CABARET

60. A friend of mine once went to a naughty cabaret show where the stripper was so ugly that when she was half-way through her act the audience shouted: 'Put them on! Put them on!'

CANNIBALS

61. One tribe of cannibals was converted by missionaries to becoming good Catholics – they ate fishermen only on Fridays.

62. One clever cannibal toasted his mother-in-law at the wedding dinner.

63. One cannibal wanted to become a detective so he could grill all his suspects.

CAROL SINGING

64. When I was younger I used to love Carol singing. Now I'm older I love Carol sighing.

CARS

65. The car was so old and dilapidated that someone scrawled on it: 'Rust in peace.'

66. The car dealer tried to sell me a car that he said was in mint condition. It had a hole in the middle.

67. I was nearly late arriving at this meeting. The journey from my home was extremely arduous and I had to walk the last few miles after I suddenly lost control of my car – the finance company re-possessed it.

68. I bought a car that was rust free. The car dealer sold me the car for two thousand pounds and didn't charge anything for all the rust.

69. A friend of mind has a car that is so old it's insured against fire, theft and Viking raids.

70. I know a man whose car is in such bad condition that when he took it to the garage and told a mechanic: 'Give it a service' – they gave it a burial service.

71. Frederick: 'My cousin thinks he's a car.'
Julia: 'What does he do?'
Frederick: 'He makes car-like noises and jogs along the road instead of the pavement. When he gets to a petrol station he pours petrol in the back pocket of his trousers.'
Julia: 'Shouldn't you do something about it?'
Frederick: 'I suppose I should, but I need the money he gives me. Every Saturday he pays me £35 to give him a good wax and polish.'

72. What is the difference between an ancient car and a class in school?
Not much – they both have lots of nuts and a crank at the front.

73. When buying an old second-hand car always insist on getting one with heated rear windows. That way, in winter you can warm your hands while you're pushing it.

CATS

74. Outraged customer: 'This cat you sold me is absolutely useless!'

Petshop owner: 'What's wrong with it? It looks perfectly all right to me.'

Outraged customer: 'When you sold it to me you promised it would be a good cat for mice. Yet every time it sees a mouse it runs away and hides.'

Petshop owner: 'Well, isn't that a good cat for mice?'

CENTIPEDE

75. One day two male centipedes were standing in the street when a female centipede strolled past.

One male centipede turned to the other and said: 'Now, there goes a nice pair of legs, pair of legs, pair of legs, pair of legs, pair of legs . . .'

CHILDREN

76. The two little girls were busy boasting to each other about how great their respective fathers were.

'*My* father had lunch with Shakespeare yesterday,' said Sally.

'But Shakespeare is dead,' commented Clare.

'Oh,' replied Sally, unperturbed. 'No wonder Dad said he was quiet.'

77. Angela's mother was looking in the mirror and plucking out the few grey hairs which she found on her head.

'Mummy, why do you have some grey hair?' inquired Angela.

'Probably because you're such a naughty girl and cause me so much worry.'

'Oh!' said Angela. 'You must have been a devil towards grandmother.'

78. A small boy was peering through a hole in the fence of a nudist colony. His friend, Paul, came up to him and asked: 'Tim, what can you see? Are they men or women in there?'

'I don't really know,' replied Tim, 'none of them have got any clothes on.'

79. Little Fred came home from school after a particularly hard day and said to his mother: 'I wish I'd lived in olden days.'

'Why?' asked his mother, curious to know the reason.

'Because then I wouldn't have so much history to learn.'

80. Simon had been warned that he must be on his best behaviour when his wealthy aunt arrived for a brief holiday visit.

It was at tea during the first day of her stay that Simon kept looking at his aunt then, when the meal was almost finished, he asked: 'Auntie, when are you going to do your trick?'

'What trick is that, dear?' she inquired.

'Well,' began Simon, 'Daddy says you can drink like a fish.'

81. Dorothy: 'Mum, did you know that Marconi was a famous inventor?'

Mother: 'Yes, dear. But it's not polite to say Ma Coni – you should say Mrs Coni.'

82. Mother: 'Where did all the jam tarts go? I only made them an hour ago and I told you not to eat them all – now there's only one left.'

Fat son: 'So? I did what you said. I didn't eat them *all* – I left one.'

83. Tommy found the old, abandoned family Bible in the attic and opened it to find a large leaf pressed between its heavy pages.

'Oh,' he said. 'Adam must have left his clothes here.'

84. Samantha was a six-year-old who liked to exaggerate almost everything she saw or did.

One day she was looking out of the window when she called to her mother: 'Mummy, Mummy! Come quickly! There's a lion walking in the road outside our house!'

Samantha's mother looked out of the window, but could only see a small ginger cat.

'Samantha! You're lying again!' she scolded. 'Go upstairs to your room immediately and pray to God for forgiveness for being such a naughty little girl – and beg him to stop you from telling so many lies.'

Samantha ran up to her room, sobbing. A short time later she came down to her mother and said: 'I've prayed to God like you said, Mummy. And He said that *He*, too, thought the ginger cat looked rather like a lion.'

85. 'Mummy,' said little Desmond, 'at school today the religious teacher kept going on about "dust to dust and ashes to ashes". What did she mean?'

'I expect it means that we all come from dust and that, in the end, we'll return to dust.'

That evening, Desmond came running down the stairs from his room, calling anxiously for his mother.

'What is it? What's the matter?' she asked.

'Mummy! Come up quickly and look under my bed. Either someone has gone or someone is just coming!'

86. Yesterday, my young daughter (we called her 'Yesterday' because she was an afterthought) asked my husband: 'Where do I come from?'

He was rather embarrassed, so he told her to ask me.

'Where do I come from?' she asked again, and so I carefully explained to her all about love, marriage, sex, the whole facts of life.

My daughter then said: 'Yes – I know all that. But where do I come from? My friend Sally comes from Cardiff – where do *I* come from?'

87. This morning my son asked me if I could tell him what makes the sky blue. I told him to look it up in an encyclopaedia.

At lunchtime he asked me how long it would take to boil an ostrich egg. I said I didn't know.

This afternoon my son asked me how far away from Earth is the planet Pluto. I said I didn't know.

Earlier this evening he asked me how deep a fathom is in metres. I said I didn't know, but he could look it up in a dictionary.

Just before I left to come to this meeting my son asked me: 'Who was the first King of England?' I said I couldn't remember.

Then he asked: 'Do you mind me asking you so many questions?'

I told him: 'Of course not.' How else will he learn things if he doesn't ask questions?

88. My youngest son thinks that a wombat is a thing you use to play wom.

89. A woman was walking in the park with eleven children following her.

'Good afternoon,' called a friendly gardener. 'Are all the children yours, or is it a picnic?'

'Unfortunately,' replied the woman, 'the children are all mine – and it's certainly no picnic.'

90. Every family should have two children. That way, if one of them becomes a poet or a painter, the other can give them financial support.

91. I once overheard a small girl talking to one of her friends: 'The way mummies and daddies and teachers are always moaning and complaining I think that's why they're called *groan*-ups.'

92. My small son showed me this morning how to make a cigarette lighter. He took most of the tobacco out of it.

93. 'Mum,' asked the small girl, 'do you mind if my exam results are like a submarine?'

'What do you mean?' asked the mother.

'Below C-level.'

94. My daughter walks very quietly whenever she's near the bathroom cabinet. She says she doesn't want to wake the sleeping pills.

95. My small son went with some friends to the local ice rink. When he returned he told me: 'I still don't know if I can skate. I can't seem to stand upright long enough to find out.'

96. It was a tough neighbourhood. Two girls, Sophie and Susan were arguing:

'*My* mother is better than *your* mother,' shouted Sophie.

'And *my* father is better than *your* father,' snapped Susan.

'Oh,' said Sophie. 'I suppose he is. Even my mum says so.'

97. I was sitting on a crowded train from Bournemouth to Waterloo when a young woman with her five children got on at Southampton. The children were all eating ice creams.

The train was so crowded there was nowhere to sit, so they stood in the narrow aisle and one of the children's ice creams kept touching the expensive fur coat of one of the seated passengers.

'Bernard!' snapped the child's mother. 'Don't hold your ice cream like that. You're getting bits of fur stuck in it.'

98. When I told my children that I used to be young once, they congratulated me on having such a long memory.

99. The house-proud woman gave birth to twins. She kept her house immaculately clean. The kitchen permanently smelt of disinfectant.

The twin's milk bottles were always thoroughly sterilized;

their clothes washed in the most powerful of washing powders to remove any germs.

Then, when the twins started to get a bit grumpy and grizzly she asked a friend who had successfully coped with triplets what she should do.

'Oh,' said the friend, 'the twins are probably just teething. Why don't you put your finger in their mouths and . . .'

'What!' shrieked the twins' mother. 'Don't you have to boil the finger first?'

100. The children where I live are so sophisticated that when they write rude words on walls they write them in ancient Greek and Latin.

101. Rebecca was going on safari in Africa with her parents during her summer holiday from school. She had to have the usual round of injections some weeks before her trip.

'Please can you put a plaster on my right arm?' Rebecca asked the nurse.

'Why?' said the nurse. 'You're right handed and so I'm giving you the injections on your left arm. Why do you want a plaster on your right arm?'

'Because,' replied Rebecca, 'I have to go back to school after you've given me the injections.'

'I know,' said the nurse. 'That's why if you have the plaster over your injection on your left arm the other children at school will know you've had an injection and so will not bang or bump into your left arm.'

'If you knew the children in my school,' said Rebecca, 'you'd know that is *exactly* why I want the plaster on the wrong arm.'

102. Wilbur had just returned from an overseas business trip and staggered home with a large, brightly wrapped parcel. He was met at the door by his five children.

'Daddy,' asked one of the children, 'what's in the parcel?'

'It's a wonderful new toy,' replied Wilbur. 'It was given to me by one of my firm's clients. The problem is, he only gave me one toy, and as there are five of you, I don't know which one of you should have the toy.'

'Can't we share it?' asked one of the children.

'I suppose you could,' agreed Wilbur, 'but it's something that can only be played with by one person at a time, so I need to work out which one of you gets to use it first. Now, which person in the family always does as Mum tells them and never answers back?'

One of the children immediately responded: 'Daddy, you'd better have first go with the toy, then.'

CHINESE

103. There is an ancient Chinese ceremony in which the parents of a child choose the baby's name.

As soon as the baby is born, all the cutlery in the house of its parents is thrown in the air. The parents then listen to the falling knives, forks, and spoons and choose a name: ping, chang, fan, fung, cheung . . .

CHRISTENING

104. When the Mexican fireman had twin sons he had them christened Jose and Hose B.

105. I once knew a couple who wanted their baby to behave during its christening and so they practised every day for a week before the service by using the kitchen sink.

CHRISTMAS

106. Every Christmas I get an awful pain that stays for a week. Then my mother-in-law goes back to her own home.

107. 'Mummy,' said the small boy, 'can I have a saluki or a dachshund for Christmas?'

'No,' replied his mother, 'you'll have what lots of other people are having – turkey.'

108. The little girl would have bought her grandmother a box of handkerchiefs for Christmas, but she couldn't do this as she said she didn't know the exact size of her grandmother's nose.

109. What do angry mice send at Christmas?
Cross mouse cards.

110. I once gave my boyfriend a pocket comb for Christmas, but he never used it. He said he didn't need to comb his pockets.

111. My husband is always moaning at me. Whatever I do, he can find something to complain about.
Last Christmas he gave me two pairs of ear-rings – one covered in plastic pearls and the other in fake diamonds.
When I put on the plastic pearl ones he said: 'What's wrong with the diamond ones? Don't you like them?'

112. I can always tell what my wife is getting me for Christmas by looking at the receipts the credit card company sends to me.

CHURCH
113. It was Christmas morning and the family were plodding home from church through the snow, discussing the service. They all seemed to have a bad word to say.
Dad thought the bells had been rung dreadfully; Mum thought that the hymns were badly chosen; the eldest son fell asleep during the sermon and his twin sister could not agree with the prayers; all except for the youngest boy who opined, 'I don't know what you are all complaining about: *I* thought it was a damn good show for a penny!'

114. The only times a lot of people go to Church is when they go to see things thrown: water at christenings, confetti and rice at weddings, and earth at funerals.

115. Just outside the church, the small boy found a one pound coin and picked it up.

The vicar saw the boy and said: 'Hello! I see you've found a coin. Are you going to keep it?'

'No, sir,' replied the boy.

'Excellent, excellent!' beamed the vicar.

'I'm going to spend it,' said the boy.

CINEMA

116. I've given up trying to see a film at the cinema. Last night I bought five separate tickets and *still* I didn't get in to see the film.

Every time I bought a ticket and went towards the film theatre a stupid man took my ticket and tore it in half – so I had to get another one. Then he would do the same to that one, too.

117. A young man was sitting in the cinema when a very fat lady got up during the interval and stepped painfully on his toes while squeezing past him into the aisle.

A short time later, the same fat lady returned, carrying an ice cream and a large packet of popcorn.

'Did I tread on your toes, young man?' she asked.

'I'm afraid you did. And you didn't apologize.'

'Good,' snapped the woman. 'Then this *is* my row.'

118. When I go to the cinema I want to be entertained. I want to see adventure stories and comedies. I *don't* want to see sex, violence and bad language – I get all that from my wife.

119. Just at the climax of an epic film an old man started grubbing around on the floor under the seats.

'What on earth are you doing?' the understandably irritated woman next to him rasped in a low voice.

'Trying to find my toffee,' said the man.

'Can't you leave it till the end? You are ruining the film,' snapped the woman.

'No!' croaked the old boy, 'It has got my false teeth stuck in it!'

CIRCUS

120. The last time I went to a circus there was a man eating penknives. He was a sword swallower on a diet.

CLEANERS

121. Office manager: 'Look at all the dust on this desk! It looks as if it hasn't been cleaned for a fortnight.'

Cleaning lady: 'Don't blame me, sir. I've only been here a week.'

CLOAKROOM ATTENDANT

122. Cloakroom attendant: 'Please leave your hat here, sir.'

Club customer: 'I don't have a hat.'

Cloakroom attendant: 'Then I'm sorry, sir, but you cannot come into the Club. I have orders that people cannot enter unless they leave their hat in the cloakroom.'

CLOCK

123. A young man purchased a large grandfather clock from an antiques shop in Brighton.

He put the unwrapped clock over his shoulder and began to look for a taxi. He hailed one approaching from the right, but it ignored him so, swinging around, he tried to flag one down approaching from the left. Unfortunately, in turning around, the clock over his shoulder struck an old lady on the head and she fell into the gutter.

'Idiot!' she shrieked. 'Why can't you wear a normal wrist-watch like the rest of us?'

COMEDIAN

124. Comedian: 'Laughter is a wonderful thing – so other comics tell me!'

COMMITTEES

125. The difference between a good committeeman and a bad committeeman is that a good one sleeps upright and a bad one sleeps horizontally.

126. The last time I sat on a committee we were presented with a plan which had two alternatives. We therefore narrowed it down to eighteen possibilities for further discussion.

COMPÈRES

127. 'After such a warm reception I can hardly wait to hear myself speak.'

128. 'Now we have that fantastic lady singer who got to the top because her dresses didn't.'

129. 'Tonight, our rock group will sing a medley of their hit.'

130. 'There's always a long queue of people at his performances – trying to get out.'

131. Compère to heckler: 'Why don't you go and take a long walk off a short pier?'

132. 'We were going to have Morris Dancing – but Morris couldn't come.'

133. 'This evening, one of the beautiful chorus girls was hammering on my dressing-room door for more than fifty minutes . . . but I wouldn't let her out.'

134. 'He's just come from playing Julius Caesar. Caesar lost.'

135. 'Our next singer lacks only two things to get to the top: talent and ambition.'

136. 'Our next musician was even musical as a baby – he played on the linoleum.'

137. 'The last time he performed his act was right after the chimpanzees' tea party, and everyone thought it was an encore.'

138. 'The only thing wrong with the show tonight is that the seats face the stage.'

139. 'Now we have a country singer. He has to sing in the country as they don't want him in the town.'

140. Compère to heckler: 'There's a bus leaving after the show, sir – please be under it!'

141. 'Next we have a group who will make you want to stamp your feet . . . all over them.'

142. 'I see there's a very posh lady in the front row of the audience tonight. She's eating her chips with her gloves on.'

143. 'Thank you for that amazing round of indifference.'

144. 'Our next singer is someone who wanted his name up in lights in every theatre in the world – so he changed his name to Exit.'

145. 'Our next comedian is so bad that when he took part in an open air show in the park twenty-three trees got up and walked out.'

146. 'Unfortunately, the actor who was to have been with us tonight has died. He caught a severe cold but, as you know, there's no curing an old ham.'

147. 'Now I'd like to introduce someone who, ten years ago, was an unknown failure. Now he's a famous failure.'

148. 'The next act are currently riding on the crest of a slump and I'm sure you'll be completely underwhelmed by them.'

149. 'I see we've got a very polite audience here tonight – they cover their mouths when they yawn.'

150. 'Now we have someone who has been practising the violin for twenty years – it was only last week that he discovered that you don't blow it.'

151. 'Our next lady singer is wearing a very nice dress. I wonder when that style will be in fashion again.'

152. 'Our next act will probably be up to our usual sub-standard.'

153. 'When I was first starting in this business I was advised to make sure that my name was always the largest in lights outside the theatre – that way people knew it was a show to avoid.'

154. 'Now we have a six-piece band – they only know six pieces.'

155. 'Our next stripper is so awful, if she was a building she'd be condemned.'

156. 'The last time this singer was here he gave a very moving performance. Everyone moved out of the theatre.'

157. 'If my parents knew I was here tonight as compère they'd be ashamed – they think I'm in prison.'

158. 'Now we have a rather portly trombonist. He could have been a violinist instead, if only he had known which chin to stick it under.'

159. 'Our next guest is that famous gossip columnist who, when she dies, will attract hundreds of thousands of people to her funeral – just to make quite sure she really *is* dead.'

160. 'Now we have a great puppeteer who broke into the business by pulling a few strings.'

161. 'This is the last time I work as a compère at this Club. My dressing room is so small every time I stand up I hit my head on the chain.'

162. 'Our next singer once insured his voice for a million dollars. I wonder what he did with the money?'

163. 'Now we have someone whom success hasn't changed at all – he's still the rotten, horrible person he always was.'

164. 'We close the show tonight with Samson – who is sure to bring the house down.'

COMPUTER DATING

165. I tried computer dating once – but it was a bit disappointing. When I took it to dinner and then a disco the computer didn't have much to say.

CONFERENCES

166. The British businessman was due to address an overseas conference, but his plane was delayed and so he had to rush straight from the airport to the conference hotel and then almost immediately had to give his speech.

While he was racing across the hotel's foyer he noticed the public toilets with the symbols of a man and a woman on the appropriate doors. He memorized the wording underneath the symbols.

Thus he began his speech with what he thought was 'Ladies and Gentlemen' in the local language. Unfortunately, his speech was not fully appreciated as he actually began by saying: 'Ladies' toilets and gentlemen's urinals. Welcome to you all.'

CONFESSIONS

167. It was a regular coffee morning at Alice's house, and her two friends had got on to the subject of confessions and were detailing their secret vices.

'My trouble,' said Sheila, 'is that I'm such a flirt. I can't get enough of men and I've lost count how many times I've been unfaithful to John.'

'My problem is gambling,' commented Barbara. 'The house-keeping money soon runs out at the betting shop and I'm in debt up to my ears. But still the lure of the horses urges me on.'

'Hmm,' said Alice. 'My secret vice is probably worse than yours – I'm such a terrible gossip.'

CONVERSATIONS

168. The best opener for any conversation is a bottle opener.

169. 'I bet I can make you talk like a Red Indian.'
'How?'
'There you are! I told you I could do it.'

170. I always know if it's a wrong number when my wife answers the phone – the conversation only lasts for twenty minutes.

171. My wife loves bitchy gossip – so does her best friend. Whenever they use the phone they speak poison to poison.

172. Whenever anyone asks me: 'Are you going to take a bath?' I always reply: 'No – I'm going to leave it where it is.'

173. Overheard at a boring party: 'Are you enjoying yourself?' to which the reply was: 'Yes, of course – what else is there to enjoy?'

174. 'Clarissa is a thief, a liar and a murderer.'
  'Oh – she must have improved since we were at school together.'

175. 'He's so unmusical he doesn't even know his brass from his oboe.'

176. 'I think she's got the makings of a star – already her head comes to a sharp point.'

177. Overheard at the blood donor clinic: 'I've come to donate a pint of blood – where do I spit it out?'

178. One response to people who like to ask: 'Is it cold out?' is to ask *them*: 'Is *what* cold out?'

179. Part of a phone conversation: 'Are you hanging up?'
  'No, I'm lying down.'

180. Overheard to a chauffeur: 'James, I'm now ninety and rather bored with life, so I want to commit suicide. Kindly drive over the next cliff.'

181. Overheard conversations: 'I don't know what to do with my hands while I'm talking.'
  'Why don't you hold them over your mouth?'

182. 'Excuse me, do you know how to pronounce "Hawaii"? Is it with a "v" sound or a "w"?'

'It's Havaii.'
'Thank you.'
'You're velcome.'

183. 'Get my broker.'
'Which one – stock or pawn?'

184. 'My old uncle has one foot in the grate.'
'Don't you mean he's got one foot in the grave?'
'No. He wants to be cremated.'

185. 'Are you trying to make a fool out of me?'
'Of course not! Why should I try to change Nature?'

186. 'Whatever I say goes.'
'Please talk to yourself.'

187. 'Which of your relations do you like best?'
'Sex.'

188. Fred: 'I've just returned from a duck shoot.'
Tom: 'How was it?'
Fred: 'Terrible! All the others shot and I had to duck.'

189. 'I'm an atheist – thank God!'

190. 'Do you have holes in your trousers?'
'No.'
'Then how do you get your legs through?'

191. 'Are you a mechanic?'
'No. I'm a MacDonald.'

192. 'You've never looked better in your life . . . whenever *that* was.'

193. 'I'm trying.'
'Yes. You're *very* trying.'

194. Shaun: 'What's in your bag?'
George: 'Chickens.'
Shaun: 'Will you give me one of them?'
George: 'No.'
Shaun: 'If I guess how many you've got in your bag, then will you give me one?'
George: 'Certainly! If you guess correctly I'll give you both.'
Shaun: 'Six.'

195. 'If God didn't want me to have any more children he wouldn't let me drink on Saturday nights.'

196. Mother: 'If you smartened yourself up you could get a job.'
Son: 'Why?'
Mother: 'Because in a job you get paid.'
Son: 'So?'
Mother: 'So then you can save some money.'
Son: 'What for?'
Mother: 'If you save enough you can eventually retire and not work any more.'
Son: 'But I'm not working now.'

COOKERY
197. 'I've prepared the turkey,' said Charles proudly to his wife. 'I've plucked it and stuffed it. All you've got to do is kill it and cook it.'

198. Two students shared a flat and a cat. Neither of the students was a particularly good cook.

One day one of the students returned to find his flatmate wringing his hands in despair.

'What happened?' asked the student.

'The cat ate your dinner?'

'Don't worry,' replied the first student. 'We'll buy another cat tomorrow.'

199. My wife is the only person I know who can ruin cornflakes – she boils them in the packet.

200. When my wife told me she'd made the chicken soup I replied: 'Good! I was worried it was for us.'

201. 'Darling,' called the young bride from the kitchen. 'I'm afraid I've spoilt your breakfast. The eggs were frying nicely when all of a sudden the shells broke and it all became very messy.'

202. My husband's cooking is so bad he's even managed to give the dustbin food poisoning.

203. 'Quite honestly, Henrietta. I shall be glad when we've eaten the last of that rhinoceros . . .'

204. 'Urrgh!' said Mr Blenkinsop, 'this lamb is tough.'
   'I'm sorry,' replied his wife, 'but the butcher said it was a spring lamb.'
   'Then that explains it,' said Mr Blenkinsop. 'I must be eating one of the springs.'

COWBOY
205. 'Say! Aren't you the rotten, horrible, wicked outlaw who held up the Northwood Stage? How's your hernia?'

CRIMINALS
206. Joe Bloggs, a small-time jewel thief, came home after robbing a nearby country house and began to saw the legs off his bed. When his wife asked him what he was doing he replied that he wanted to 'lie low for a while'.

CRUISE
207. My wife and I have recently returned from a luxury cruise.

On our first day at sea we received a note from the captain asking us to sit with him at dinner.

We didn't join him as my wife thought it was outrageous that we should pay a small fortune to go on the cruise and then be expected to eat with the staff.

CUSTOMS

208. A customs officer at Kennedy Airport, New York, opened the suitcase of a beautiful young girl from England and discovered six pairs of very brief panties. He took them out of the case for further inspection (in the vain hope of finding some concealed drugs) and found that the panties were each labelled with one day of the week, from Monday to Saturday.

'And on Sunday?' he inquired.

The girl blushed.

The next person to be inspected by the customs officer was an enormously fat woman from Montreal, and the customs officer took out twelve pairs of giant-size bloomers from her suitcase. Before he could say anything, the Montreal lady smirked, patted his arm playfully and said: 'January, February, March, April, May . . .'

D

DANCING

209. There's only two things wrong with my husband's dancing – his left foot and his right foot.

DECORATORS

210. When I told the Irish decorators that I wanted a matt finish on the walls they nailed the carpets to them.

DEFINITIONS

211. Aperitif: a pair of French false teeth.

212. Apricots: beds for baby apes.

213. Assets: baby donkeys.

214. Booby trap: a bra that is too small and too tight.

215. Derange: de place where de cowboys ride home to.

216. Disgruntled: a pig that has lost its voice.

217. Impale: to put in a bucket.

218. Inkling: a small bottle of ink.

219. Minister of Defence: a man who is always ready to lay down *your* life for *his* country.

220. Operator: a person who hates opera.

221. Pigtail: a story about a pig.

222. Politics: sounds coming from a parrot that has swallowed a watch.

223. Polygon: a dead parrot.

224. Polymath: a parrot that likes mathematics.

225. Triplets: small journeys.

DENTIST

226. The beautiful young lady in the dentist's chair was nervously wringing her hands. 'Oh dear,' she said, 'I'm so nervous. It's so frightening. I think I'd rather have a baby than my teeth seen to.'

'Well,' replied the dentist, 'which would you like the most – just let me know and I'll adjust the chair – and my clothes – accordingly.'

227. 'I went to the dentist this morning.'

'Does your tooth still hurt?'

'I don't know – the dentist kept it.'

DIETS

228. Mrs Grunge: 'Doctor, it's about this bananas-only diet you've put me on.'

Doctor: 'What about it?'

Mrs Grunge: 'It seems to be having rather a peculiar effect on me.'

Doctor: 'Oh, I wouldn't say that, Mrs Grunge. Now, if you'll just stop scratching and come down from the curtains perhaps . . .'

229. Worried young girl: 'Doctor, this new diet you've put me on makes me feel so passionate and sexy that I got carried away last night and bit off my boyfriend's right ear.'

Doctor: 'Don't worry, it's only about forty to fifty calories.'

230. Mavis: 'My doctor put me on a new diet, using more corn and other vegetable oils.'

Beryl: 'Does it work?'

Mavis: 'Well, I'm not any thinner yet – but I don't squeak any more.'

231. When I went on a diet of baked beans and garlic all I lost was ten friends.

DIVORCE

232. A friend of mine has just got divorced due to incompatibility. He had no income and his wife had no pat-ability.

233. In olden days England the unfaithful princess was divorced because she had lots of sleepless knights.

234. A couple I used to know recently got divorced and they fought over the custody of their teenage children – neither of them wanted custody.

DOCTOR

235. A woman went to her doctor to complain that her husband's sexual feelings for her seemed to have declined.

The doctor, being an old friend of the family, gave the woman some pills to slip into her husband's tea so that at least the man wouldn't get a complex about being a bit underpowered.

Two days later, the woman was back in the doctor's surgery.

'What happened?' asked the doctor. 'Did the pills work?'

'Fantastic!' replied the woman. 'I was so eager to see their effects on my husband that I tipped three of them into a cup of coffee and, within seconds of drinking it, he got up, kicked over the table and pulled me down on to the floor and ravished me.'

'Oh!' said the doctor. 'I hope you weren't too surprised?'

'Surprised?' said the woman. 'I'll never be able to set foot in the restaurant again . . .'

236. I tried to follow my doctor's advice and give up smoking cigarettes and try chewing gum instead – but the matches kept getting stuck and the gum wouldn't light.

237. Last week my friend, Mabel, was feeling terribly ill so her husband phoned the doctor's surgery.

'I'm afraid the doctor is busy until 10am Thursday,' said the receptionist.

'But that's three days away! My wife is terribly ill,' pleaded Mabel's husband. 'What if she's dead by then?'

'Well,' replied the receptionist, 'you can always phone and cancel the appointment.'

238. 'Doctor, doctor! How can I get this ugly mole off my face?'

'Get your dog to chase it back into its hole.'

239. Before I went off to India for my summer holidays I asked my doctor how I could avoid getting a disease from biting insects. He just told me not to bite any.

240. When I asked my doctor to give me something to sharpen my appetite he just gave me a razor blade.

241. Handsome young doctor: 'Say "ah!"'

Pretty young girl: 'That's a change! Most young men want me to say "yes".'

242. 'Doctor, I wish to protest about the spare part surgery operation you did on me.'

'What's wrong? I gave you another hand when your own was smashed up at your factory.'

'I know. But you gave me a female hand which is very good most of the time – it's only that whenever I go to the toilet it doesn't want to let go.'

243. As the doctor said to his girlfriend: 'I love you with all my heart – and my kidneys, liver, epiglottis, spinal cord . . .'

244. The pretty nurse explained her problem to the doctor: 'Every time I take a man's pulse it goes up. What should I do?'

'Blindfold them,' replied the doctor.

245. 'Doctor, doctor! I keep thinking I'm a pair of curtains.'

'Well, pull yourself together.'

246. Henry's doctor told him to be like a rabbit and eat lots of carrots to improve his eyesight, so he could see better at night in his work as a night watchman. His eyesight improved slightly, but he kept tripping over his ears.

247. Mrs Smith: 'Doctor, please can you help me? I've had twelve children and I'm pregnant again and I don't want any more kids after this one. I desperately need a hearing aid.'

Doctor: 'A hearing aid? What do you want a hearing aid for? Surely you want some birth control pills or some form of contraceptive device?'

Mrs Smith: 'No, doctor, I definitely want a hearing aid. You see, my husband gets drunk every Friday night and comes lumbering into my bed and says to me: "Do you want to go to sleep or what?" Me being a bit deaf I always say: "What?"'

248. 'Doctor, is there something wrong with my heart?'

'I've given you a thorough examination and I can confidently say that your heart will last as long as you live.'

249. Doctor: 'Well, Mrs Cuthbert, I haven't seen you for a long time.'

Mrs Cuthbert: 'I know, doctor. But I've been ill.'

250. 'Doctor, doctor! My small son has just swallowed a roll of film.'

'Don't worry. Let him rest a bit and we'll wait and see what develops.'

251. Since I had treatment by a private doctor I've lost five kilos in weight. The doctor's bill was so enormous I've been unable to afford to buy any food to eat.

252. Last Tuesday I was in the doctor's waiting room and a young man came in with an expensive watch for the doctor.

'Thank you, thank you, thank you!' said the man, giving the doctor the expensive watch. 'This is a small token of my thanks for all your excellent treatment of my uncle.'

'But he died last week,' said the doctor.

'I know,' replied the young man. 'Thanks to your treatment I've just inherited five million pounds.'

253. 'Doctor, doctor! I feel like a piano.'

'Then I'd better take some notes.'

254. 'Doctor, it's impossible for my wife to be pregnant. I'm a sailor and I've been away from her working on my ship overseas for more than a year.'

'I know. But it's what we call a "grudge pregnancy". Someone had it in for you.'

255. 'Doctor, doctor, I was playing my mouth-organ and I suddenly swallowed it.'

'Well, look on the bright side – you could have been playing a grand piano.'

256. When I told the doctor's receptionist that I kept thinking I was a billiard ball she told me to get to the end of the cue.

257. Yesterday I was in the doctor's waiting room and I heard a 96-year-old man pleading with the doctor for a lower sex drive.

'Surely you're imagining things,' said the doctor. 'You're 96 years old. Isn't all the feeling for sex just in your head?'

'Yes,' replied the elderly man, 'that's why I want you to lower my sex drive to the place where it might do more good.'

258. Patient: 'Doctor, doctor! I've just swallowed a whole sheep.'

Doctor: 'How do you feel?'

Patient: 'Quite baa-d.'

259. This morning I went to the doctor to see if he had a cure for my wife's sinus trouble. Every time she drags me out shopping she keeps telling me 'sign us' for this, 'sign us' for that.

260. The woman went to see the doctor. She had a large flower growing out of the top of her head.

The doctor looked at the flower and said: 'That is quite remarkable. I've never seen anything like that before. But I'll soon cut it off.'

'Cut it off?' snapped the woman. 'I don't want the flower cut off. I just want it treated against greenfly.'

261. While I was in the doctor's waiting room there was this tiny man only about six inches tall. Although he was there before me, he let me see the doctor first. I suppose he just had to be a little patient.

262. 'Doctor, doctor! Can you help me? My tongue keeps sticking out.'

'That's good. Now, if you can just lick these stamps . . .'

263. I went to the doctor this morning and told him I felt run down.

'Why do you feel that?" he asked.

'Because,' I replied, 'I've got tyre marks on my legs.'

264. Patient: 'Doctor, every time I eat fruit I get this strange urge to give people all my money.'

Doctor: 'Would you like an apple or a banana?'

265. When the doctor came to visit my aunt Claudette my aunt said: 'Doctor, I hope you're going to tell me that I'm very ill.'

The doctor looked at my aunt and said: 'But why? Don't you want me to say you're very healthy?'

'No,' replied aunt Claudette. 'I feel absolutely terrible. And I don't want to feel like this if I'm healthy. But I'm sure you can make me better.'

266. After some months of marriage, a girl wrote the following letter to her doctor:

'Dear Doctor,

Since I got married, my husband seems to have gone mad. He is after me at breakfast, coffee break, lunchtime – even tea time – and then all night every few hours. Is there anything I can do or give to help him? I await your kind reply.

P.S.: Please excuse shaky handwriting.'

267. When the young man was being examined by the doctor he was asked: 'Does it burn when you pee in the toilet?'

'I don't know,' replied the young man, 'I don't think I'd dare hold a match to it.'

268. The man went to see his doctor because he was feeling under the weather. The doctor asked the usual questions, such as had the man been drinking or eating too much.

'No,' said the man.

'Well, perhaps you have had too many late nights?' queried the doctor.

'No,' the man replied.

The doctor thought about the problem for a while and then

asked 'Much sex?'

'Infrequently,' came the reply.

'Is that two words or one?'

269. It was three o'clock in the morning and the plumber's telephone rang. It was the doctor, saying that his toilet seemed to have broken and could the plumber come immediately to fix it.

The plumber reluctantly agreed to visit the doctor's house, although the plumber warned his client that at this time of night he could only expect him to provide 'a doctor's treatment.'

When he arrived, the plumber went straight to the offending toilet, threw an aspirin down it, and then said to the doctor: 'If it's not better by lunchtime tomorrow, phone me and I'll come again.'

270. Patient: 'Doctor, I've got diarrhoea.'

Doctor: 'Yes. It runs in your family.'

271. Doctor: 'Take three teaspoonfuls of this medicine after each meal.'

Patient: 'But I've only got two teaspoons.'

272. Patient: 'Doctor, I keep thinking I'm a ball of string.'

Doctor: 'Well, go and get knotted.'

273. 'Doctor, I've got wind – can you give me anything for it?'

'How about a kite?'

274. Old man: 'Doctor, how do I stand?'

Doctor: 'That's what puzzles me.'

275. Doctor: 'Miss Smith, you have acute appendicitis.'

Miss Smith: 'I came here to be examined – not admired.'

276. The doctor was visiting 78-year-old Jim at his home to give him a routine check-up.

'For a man of your age,' said the doctor, 'you're in excellent shape. How do you manage it?'

'Well,' replied Jim, 'I don't drink, I don't smoke and I've never played around with women and . . .'

He was interrupted by a crashing sound and female shrieks coming from the room immediately above them.

'What was that?' asked the doctor.

'Oh!' said Jim, 'only my father chasing the new au pair girl. He must be drunk again!'

277. Two doctors in the USA were talking.

1st doctor: 'Why did you perform that operation on Mrs Weitzman?'

2nd doctor: 'Twenty thousand dollars.'

1st doctor: 'No. Perhaps you didn't hear me correctly. What did Mrs Weitzman have?'

2nd doctor: 'Twenty thousand dollars.'

DOGS

278. Our house is so small I had to train the dog to wag its tail up and down instead of from side-to-side.

279. One day I'd like to have enough courage to say to people who keep telling me that their pet dog is just like one of the family: 'Oh – which one is it like?'

280. Fred: 'We've got a new dog. Would you like to come and play with him?'

Tom: 'I've heard him barking and growling. He sounds very fierce and unfriendly. Does he bite?'

Fred: 'That's what I want to find out.'

281. 'I washed my dog last night and he died.'

'Died? But why? Washing a dog can't kill it.'

'Well, it was either the washing or the spin drying that did it.'

282. Timothy: 'I say, your dog is very clever being able to play the trombone.'

Algernon: 'Not really – he can't read a single note of music.'

283. Albert has got the laziest dog in the world. Even when he's watering his garden the dog refuses to lift a leg to help.

284. 'What is your dog's name?'

'I don't know. He refuses to tell me.'

285. My dog is a doberman pincher. Every time he sees a doberman he pinches it.

286. When Poole and Bournemouth introduced bye-laws to ban dogs from certain parts of the beach and to fine their owners if the dogs fouled public places, a friend of mine decided that she had better train her dog to go to the toilet in the gutter. This was rather difficult, as the dog kept falling off the roof.

287. A friend of mine keeps making films about canine creatures – they are all *dog*umentaries.

288. What noise do you get if you cross a cocker spaniel with a poodle and a cockerel?

A cockerpoodledoo.

289. I've just come from an awkward meeting with my next-door neighbour. He's almost seven feet tall and has a huge Alsatian dog.

Unfortunately, the dog kept leaping at the garden fence so much that it made a hole in it and got into my garden. That was when it happened. My little cat killed the big Alsatian.

'How did your puny cat kill Big Al, my dog?' demanded my neighbour.

'I'm sorry,' I said, 'but my cat stuck in your dog's throat and he choked to death.'

DREAMS

290. Young man: 'Darling, I dreamt about you last night.'
Pretty young girl: 'Did you?'
Young man: 'No – you wouldn't let me!'

DRINK

291. I asked my wife to give me a stiff drink and she put starch in my tea.

292. A large man with an enormous beer belly went into his usual pub, asked for a pint of beer, and then took a mirror out of his pocket.

'What are you going to do with the mirror?' asked the barmaid, as the man propped the mirror up on the bar counter.

'Look in it,' replied the man, sipping his pint of beer. 'My doctor told me today that I have to watch my drinking.'

293. At the bar last night was a man who demanded to be served a drink called Less.

'I've never heard of it,' said the barmaid.

'But you *must* have,' insisted the man.

'We don't have it. Is Less a new foreign beer or something? Where did you hear about it?' asked the barmaid.

'I don't exactly know what it is,' replied the man, 'but my doctor insists that I should drink Less.'

DRIVERS

294. When the professor of mathematics was involved in a car crash he was asked by a policeman if he could remember the other car's registration number.

'Not exactly,' replied the professor, 'but the total of the numbers divided by the last digit was equal to the square root of the second number.'

295. I was on a walk in Dorset, lost in thought, when a car pulled up beside me and a fat gentleman wound down his car window and shouted: 'Yokel! Do you know the way to Bournemouth?'

'Yes,' I replied, and continued walking.

296. The sports car came hurtling down the narrow, winding country lane, narrowly avoiding an elderly lady in an old car.

'Pig!' shouted the elderly lady as the sports car driver scraped past her car.

'Bitch!' shouted back the sports car driver as he drove on and around the corner – and hit a pig in the middle of the road.

297. Policeman: 'Madam, I have just recorded you as 50 at least.'

Female speeding motorist: 'Don't be ridiculous, officer! These clothes always make me look a lot older.'

DRUNKS

298. The drunk was staggering along the street when he was stopped by a policeman.

'Excuse me, sir,' said the policeman, 'but where are you going?'

'I'm going to a lec . . . lecture,' replied the drunk.

'Who is giving the lecture?' asked the policeman.

'Wh . . . when I . . . when I g . . . get home,' said the drunk, 'my wife will give me the lecture.'

299. It was a dark, cloudy night and the drunk staggered into the cemetery and fell into a hole which had been dug in preparation for a burial the following day. The drunk hiccuped and fell asleep.

Half an hour later another drunk swayed into the cemetery. He was singing loudly and his raucous voice woke up the drunk in the grave who suddenly started to yell that he was cold.

The singing drunk tottered to the edge of the grave and

peered blurrily down at the complaining drunk. 'It's no wonder you're cold,' he shouted down to the drunk, 'you've kicked all the soil off yourself.'

E

300. My employer is the sort of man who grows on you – like warts.

301. The managing director of a large company – which he had founded – received a short job application letter for the position of assistant managing director from a young man who detailed his education at a top public school, outlined his aristocratic background and intentions of marrying the daughter of a duke – yet failed to give any indication of his competency or even knowledge of the job available.

The managing director therefore felt obliged to write back to the young man: 'Dear Sir, Thank you for applying for the position advertised. I am unable to employ you since we require the services of someone for managerial rather than breeding purposes.'

302. Boss: 'I don't like "yes" men. When I say "no" I want them to say "no" too.'

303. Our boss is so popular everybody wants to work for him – the local undertaker, the grave-digger . . .

304. My boss is so mean that whenever he pays anyone a compliment he insists on a receipt.

305. My boss thinks very highly of me. Today he even called me a perfect nonentity.

306. We don't know what to get our boss for Christmas. What do you get for someone who's had everybody?

307. The managing director looked around the board room after making his speech in favour of a particular course of action.

'Now,' he said, 'we'll take a vote on my recommendations. All those in opposition raise your right arm and say "I resign".'

308. You can't help admiring our boss. If you don't, you don't work here any more.

309. The only reason my boss never says an unkind remark about anyone is because he only ever talks about himself.

F

FAIRY TALES

310. 'Mummy, why do fairy tales always start "Once Upon a Time"?'

'They don't always my dear. The ones your father tells usually start with "I got caught up at the office; sorry I'm late love . . .".'

FAMILY TREE

311. One woman paid a genealogist five thousand pounds to trace her family tree – then she had to pay another five thousand to have it hushed up.

FARMERS

312. Farmer Jim was very worried about the poor performance of his prize bull for which he had paid an astronomical sum. He talked to all his friends every time he went to the market and one day learned from a cousin that there was an amazing vet way down in the West Country.

He was so depressed about the bull that he decided this last resort was the answer and he took himself off to Cornwall to find the vet. At last he found the chap who urged him to give his bull a great big pill once a day.

A few months later he met his cousin who asked him how he had got on. 'Oh, it was marvellous,' he said, 'he gave me these pills for the bull and I had no sooner started him off on them than he hit the jackpot. In fact,' he said, 'I am making a fortune out of the local farmers – they can't get their cows round here fast enough!'

'What are these pills then?' asked his cousin.

'Oh!' said Farmer Jim, 'huge great green jobs like bombs, with a peppermint taste!'

313. Wealthy poultry farmer, Bernard Nurnberg, of Tucson, Arizona was over in the UK on a turkey safari, looking for new ways to boost his production. He arrived at a small farm near Ballachulish and announced himself to the diminutive Scots farmer, Hamish McTavish:

'The name's Nurnberg, Bernard Nurnberg,' he warbled, shaking the Scotsman's hand vigorously. 'I'm here to find out how you raise turkeys right here in Scotland. How large is your farm?'

'Och well,' said Hamish, 'if you look down the burn on your left that is my left-hand boundary. Where you see the woods in the distance is my bottom boundary. Now here on the right-hand side is a wee "tump", as we call it in Scotland (which just means a small hill) and if you look where we have burnt the heather in a long line along the side of the hill, that is my right-hand boundary. The roadway where you have just come in completes the square so really, when you are standing here, you can see the lot.'

'Oh my,' drawled Bernard, 'compared to my estate in Arizona this is just a side-show! Why back home it takes three days just to drive my truck around the perimeter!'

'Is *that* so?' rejoined Hamish, and after a thoughtful pause, 'It will be some years now I suppose, since *I* had a truck like *that*!'

314. One farmer I know is trying to cross a cow with an octopus. He wants to breed a creature that can milk itself.

FILM CREDITS
315. Costumes designed by Plaster of Paris.

316. Lion tamer: Claude Bottom.

317. Tents supplied by Marquee de Sade.

FIRE

318. The house was on fire. A woman appeared at an upstairs window. She was clutching a baby and screaming: 'My baby! My baby! Save my baby!'

'Throw the baby down to me!' shouted a young man. 'I'll catch him.'

'You might drop him,' shouted the woman.

'I'm a professional footballer,' shouted the man 'I'm a goalkeeper. I'm very good at catching. The baby will be safe with me.'

The woman threw down the baby to the young man who put all his professional expertise into operation, and he expertly caught the baby and then, unthinkingly, kicked it over the garden wall.

319. Man on phone: 'Help! Come quickly! My house is on fire!'

Fire brigade officer: 'How do we get to your house?'

Man on phone: 'What? Don't you still have those big red trucks?'

FISHING

320. Last weekend I did something I've never done before – I went fly fishing: and caught a three ounce fly!

FOOD

321. Rhubarb always seems to look like rather embarrassed celery.

322. 'I still feel rather sick,' said Barbara to her best friend.

'Do you know what caused it?' asked the friend.

'I think it must have been the oysters I ate last night,' said Barbara.

'Were they bad?' asked the friend. 'What did they look like when you opened them?'

'Oh!' said Barbara. 'You mean you're supposed to *open* them before you eat them?'

323. I once saw a man eat a pocket watch. Then he swallowed two wristwatches. He said I could stay and see him swallow even more watches – but I said I thought it was very time consuming.

324. 'I'm going to eat a pet,' said the small girl to her brother.

'You can't do that!' protested the brother. 'It's cruel and they will taste horrible.'

'I *am* going to eat a pet,' insisted the sister, defiantly.

The boy was almost in tears as he asked his sister: 'Is it the kitten or the puppy you're going to eat?'

'Neither,' replied the sister. 'The pet I'm going to eat is a crumpet!'

FOOTBALL

325. 'Dad, dad!' said Gareth. 'I think I've been selected for the school football team.'

'That's good,' replied Gareth's father. 'But why do you only *think* you've been selected? Aren't you sure? What position will you play?'

'Well,' said Gareth, 'it's not been announced officially, but I overheard the football coach tell my teacher that if I was in the team I'd be a great draw-back.'

326. My wife and son were watching a football match on TV when my son got excited and shouted: 'Pass the ball! Pass the ball! Why won't the idiot pass the ball to Smith?'

'Well,' said my wife, 'you can't really expect a footballer who cost a million pounds to pass the ball to a player who cost a lot less.'

327. When I was a young boy all the other kids insisted that I was in the football team. They said I was vital to the game. They couldn't possibly play without me. They needed me. I was the only one with a football.

FORTUNE TELLING

328. My husband wanted his fortune told, but didn't know whether to go to a mindreader or a palmist. I told him to go to a palmist – at least we know he's got a palm.

329. A young girl visits a clairvoyant, who, looking into her crystal ball, bursts out laughing. With a crack like a pistol shot, the girl slaps the medium hard across the jaw.

'*Ouch!* What was *that* for?' protests the fortune teller.

'My mother always insists that I should strike a happy medium!' the child explains.

330. 'I've heard that you are an excellent fortune teller. Can you predict the next few months?'

'Certainly! December, January, February.'

G

GARDENING

331. My wife, Virginia, likes to talk to the plants in the garden. So far, only one of them talks back and is always saying things like: 'You're wonderful, beautiful. Thank you for looking after me in the garden. You're fantastic!'

I suppose this was only to be expected of a plant called Virginia Creeper!

GHOSTS

332. The father ghost told his son: 'Spook only when you are spoken to.'

333. Richard was not very frightened when he saw the ghost and, since it appeared to be friendly, he asked the ghost if he could try to photograph it.

The ghost willingly agreed and Richard went to fetch his camera, but found that the flash attachment on it was broken.

The spirit was willing – but the flash was weak.

334. Then there was the ghost who didn't believe in people.

335. Human: 'Do you plan to stay in this town very long?'
Ghost: 'No – I'm only passing through.'

336. The young ghost got very scared when his friends told him too many human stories.

337. It was a graveyard romance. Boy meets ghoul.

338. Some years ago I tried to become a ghost writer. But I couldn't find any ghosts who wanted me to write for them.

339. Where do ghosts take their dirty coats?
  To a dry-screamers.

340. What did the phantom on guard duty outside the haunted castle say when he heard a noise?
  'Halt! Who ghosts there?'

341. Why was the shy ghost frightened of going to the opticians' party?
  Because he thought he might make a spooktacle of himself.

342. What do you call a female ghost who serves drinks and food on a plane?
  An air ghostess.

343. What music do ghosts like?
  Haunting melodies.

344. How did the two ghosts fall in love?
  It was love at first fright.

345. On what day do ghosts play tricks on each other?
  April Ghoul's Day.

346. Where can you catch a ghost train?
  At a manifestation.

347. Why did the female ghoul like demons?

Because demons are a ghoul's best friend.

GIRLFRIENDS

348. My new girlfriend is like a grapefruit. Whenever I squeeze her she spits at me.

349. 'I thought you said your new girlfriend was a model? With the greatest of respect, she doesn't really look like one. What does she model?'
    'Halloween masks.'

350. My girlfriend is a real sex object. Whenever I mention sex she objects.

351. I asked another girl I went out with if she liked nuts, and she replied: 'Why? Do you want me to marry you?'

352. My girlfriend says she only weighs eight stones – but I reckon the stones must be the size of boulders.

353. My girlfriend is one of twins. It would be quite difficult to tell them apart – if my girlfriend didn't have a moustache.

354. My girlfriend can never understand why her brother has five sisters and she only has four.

355. When someone asked my girlfriend if she ever had much trouble making up her mind, she said: 'I'm not sure. Maybe yes. Maybe no.'

356. This morning I bought my girlfriend a sexy new night-dress. Tonight I'll try and talk her out of it.

357. My girlfriend speaks Italian like a native – a native from Scunthorpe.

358. I'll never forget my first girlfriend. It was real puppy love. Every time I went to kiss her she said 'Woof!'

GOAT

359. I once knew a man who thought he was a goat. He'd believed that ever since he was a young kid.

GOLDFISH

360. 'Why haven't you changed the water in the goldfish bowl like I asked you to do?'

'Because they haven't drunk the first lot yet.'

GOLF

361. Mrs Brown was fed up with her husband being forever out of the house and playing golf.

'Why can't you stay at home a bit more?' she asked.

'Because it's fun on the golf course,' replied her husband. 'And it's good exercise.'

'Maybe I should try it, too?' suggested Mrs Brown.

'You probably wouldn't like it,' said Mr Brown. 'All the walking might tire you out. Why don't you stay at home with your knitting and the TV?'

But Mrs Brown insisted her husband took her to the golf club and gave her lessons.

The very first day together on the course, her husband's first shot was appalling, but he told his wife: 'There! That's how to hit the ball. Another two or three strokes and that'll be it.'

Mrs Brown then took her first ever shot – and scored a hole in one.

Mr Brown was amazed. He was speechless.

The couple walked over to where the ball nestled in the hole and Mrs Brown said: 'That wasn't very good, was it? It's going to be very difficult to hit the ball out of this little hole.'

GOSSIP
362. If you can't repeat gossip – what else can you do with it?

H

HAIR STYLE

363. 'Do you like my new hair style?' cooed the trendy young girl to her somewhat conservative boyfriend.

'Well,' he said. 'It reminds me of a beautiful Italian dish.'

'An actress?' she inquired eagerly.

'No. Spaghetti.'

HAIRDRESSERS

364. A successful young 'Tycoon Designate' was enjoying the full works at a fancy hairdressing salon in the West End.

'Dressing, sir?' asked the barber.

'No, no!' came the swift reply. 'My wife might think I had been to a brothel.'

Unknown to him, his boss was also making an incognito visit to the high class establishment. When he was asked the same question he came out in fine voice for the benefit of his unsuspecting executive, who was still receiving a nail manicure, 'Yes, please, pile it on if you like. My wife has no idea of the smell you find in a brothel!'

HARD TIMES

365. Lord and Lady Dross-Plott had fallen on hard times.

'We must make some economies,' said the Lord. 'Couldn't you have some cookery lessons? Then you could do all our meals and we wouldn't have to continue employing the cook.'

'Only if you would have some lessons, too,' replied Lady Dross-Plott. 'If you had some sex lessons then I wouldn't need the butler and we could dispense with him, too.'

HAT

366. Charles used to wear a pork pie hat, but he got fed up with the gravy running down his neck.

HOLIDAYS

367. The young man was on his first ever holiday abroad. As he lay on the beach in a crowded part of Spain, a gorgeous young woman lay down beside him and kept making admiring glances at him.

Eventually, she said: 'I like the look of you. Would you like to come back to my apartment for a little game?'

'Fantastic!' replied the young man. 'I was just wondering where I'd find a snooker table.'

368. The Chinese girl had just returned to Singapore from a holiday in England and was talking to her best friend.

'Mabel, I've been thinking about Keith ever since I left England. Now I'm back home I don't think I should write to him as our friendship was only slight.'

'But, Wendy, you promised to marry him!'

'I know. But that was all.'

369. A beautiful young girl was lying, asleep, in a tiny bikini immediately below the promenade. A small boy accidentally dropped a piece of his vanilla ice-cream on her, and it landed on her navel.

The girl immediately awoke and sprang to her feet, shocked, and said: 'These seagulls must live in a flipping refrigerator.'

370. Timothy was on holiday in Ireland and staying at a small country inn.

One evening in the bar he was amazed by the following conversation:

'That's a beautiful hat you've got there,' said an old man to a young fellow who was standing next to him at the bar. 'Where did you buy it?'

'At O'Grady's,' replied the young man.

'Why, I go there myself!' commented the old man. 'You must be from around these parts, then?'

'Aye. From Murphy Street.'

'Gracious!' exclaimed the old man. 'I live there, too!'

'Quite amazing,' commented Timothy to the barman, 'that those two folk over there live in the same street and have only just met.'

'Don't you believe it!' said the barman. 'They're actually father and son but they're always too drunk to recognize each other.'

371. 'Help, help!' shouted the man in the sea. 'I can't swim.'

'So what?' shouted back a drunk from the shore. 'I can't play the piano, but I'm not shouting about it.'

372. Mr and Mrs Smith and Mr and Mrs Brown had known each other for many years and frequently went on holiday together.

This year Mr Smith suggested to Mr Brown that to add spice to their holiday, perhaps they should exchange partners. Mr Brown considered this for a moment, then agreed it was a good idea, and both men got their wives to agree, too.

Thus it was that after their first night in Malta, Mr Brown turned to his holiday partner in bed and said: 'That was certainly exciting and different.'

'Yes, I agree,' said his partner, Mr Smith.

373. Mother, in holiday apartment: 'Sarah, can you wash up the dishes?'

Sarah: 'But we don't have any rubber gloves. You know water isn't very good for my skin.'

Mother: 'Is that why you've spent most of the day in the sea?'

HONEYMOONS

374. 'Darling, just imagine – we've now been married for twenty-four hours.'

'Yes, dear, it's incredible. And it seems only as if it was yesterday.'

375. Cuthbert married a very refined virgin from an impeccable background, and took her away to Tunis for their honeymoon.

On the first night in their hotel, Cuthbert quickly stripped off his clothes and jumped into bed and then watched while his wife slowly removed all her garments.

But Cuthbert was rather surprised when she clambered into bed completely naked except for her white gloves.

'Why don't you take your gloves off?' he asked.

'Because mummy said I might actually have to *touch* the beastly thing,' she replied.

376. It was in olden days and the bride and groom were setting off alone on their honeymoon – travelling by horse and carriage.

Suddenly, the horse reared up, startled by a snake in its path. Annoyed at the horse's behaviour, the man waved his finger threateningly at the horse and said: 'That's your first warning.'

They continued their journey until about half an hour later when the horse stopped at a water trough at the roadside to drink a few sips of water.

Again, the man was annoyed at this interruption in their journey, and he wagged his finger and said, menacingly: 'That's the second warning.'

They continued their journey until dusk, when again the horse reared up, rocking the carriage violently. The man clambered down from the carriage, took out his gun, and shot the horse dead between its eyes, saying as he did this: 'And that was the third time.'

The man's wife, on seeing this, burst into tears. 'What did you shoot the horse for? She was probably frightened by another snake or something similar. It wasn't her fault. Now you've killed her! How could you be so cruel! If I'd known you were such a sadist I'd never have married you! How could you do it to such a poor defenceless creature?'

As she began to cry uncontrollably, her husband wagged his finger at her and said: 'That's the first warning.'

377. The 79-year-old British knight had just married a sweet, innocent 17-year-old debutante.

'Tell me, my dear,' said the knight, 'did your mother explain to you the facts of life?'

'No, sir, I'm afraid she did not.'

'Oh, how awkward,' commented the knight. 'I seem to have forgotten them.'

378. Groom: 'Would you be very annoyed with me if I confess that all my upper teeth are false?'

Bride: 'Not at all, darling. At least I can now relax and take off my wig, inflatable bra, glass eye and artificial leg.'

379. The spry old gentleman of 89 had just returned from his honeymoon with his 23-year-old bride.

'How did the honeymoon go?' asked a friend.

'Oh, it went quite well,' replied the old man, 'but did you ever try to get a marshmallow into a kid's piggy bank?'

380. As they lay in bed on the first day of their honeymoon, John turned to his wife and sighed: 'Darling, I hope you can put up with my ugly face for the rest of your life.'

'That's all right, dear,' she replied. 'You'll be out at work all day.'

HORSES

381. 'How is your yearling coming along?' one gentleman

asked another as they chatted in the Silver Ring at Ascot.

'It died,' said the other.

'That must have lost you a fortune, with the training fees and everything,' sympathized the first man.

'No, I made a profit actually,' the owner chuckled. 'I raffled him at £10 a ticket.'

'Didn't anyone sue you for fraud?'

'No. The winner got a bit shirty but I sent *him* his money back!'

382. Two thickies bought themselves a horse each and decided to keep them in the same field.

'How shall we tell which horse is which?' asked Paul.

'I'll tie a blue ribbon to the tail of my horse,' replied Rene.

Unfortunately, the ribbon on Paul's horse fell off one day in Paul's absence, so the two were again faced with the problem of deciding which horse was which.

'I know,' suggested Paul, 'you have the brown horse and I'll have the white one.'

HOSPITAL

383. I've just come out of hospital. I was in there for six weeks as a result of my boyfriend throwing me over. He caught me out with another man and threw me over a cliff.

384. Stockbroker patient: 'Tell me, nurse, what is my temperature?'

Nurse: 'A hundred and one.'

Stockbroker patient: 'When it gets to a hundred and two – sell.'

385. Frederick's wife was a surgeon, and so when Frederick had to go into hospital for an operation, she insisted on doing the surgery. She said she didn't want anyone else to open her male.

386. Bernard was walking along the street one day when a young man rushed up to him and said: 'Can you show me the quickest way to get to the hospital?'

So Bernard pushed the young man under a bus.

387. There I was, lying ill in hospital, and my husband came into the room to read to me – my insurance policies and last will and testament.

388. A friend of mine recently went into hospital for an organ transplant. Now his body can play all the hymns in the church.

389. The phone rings and matron answers the phone: 'Yes. Hello. You want to know how Mr Gough is doing? His operation seemed to go extremely well and we have every hope that he can leave the hospital soon. Might I know who is speaking so I can pass on your interest and concern to him?'

The voice on the phone answers: 'This *is* Mr Gough. They don't tell patients themselves *anything* in this place!'

390. There was a very high pitched scream from the operating theatre, and then the doctor's voice could be heard: 'Nurse! I said take off the patient's *spec*tacles.'

391. Molly, one of the nurses in the hospital, was always going around joking and laughing and teasing the patients.

Knowing Molly's sense of fun, one of the male patients named John decided to play a little trick on her.

When asked to provide a specimen of his urine he took some orange squash which his mother had brought for him and poured this into the bottle instead.

When Molly came to collect the sample, John made as if to hand the bottle over to her – but then said: 'Hmm. It looks a bit weak. I'd better pass it through again.'

He then put the bottle to his lips and drank the contents. Molly fainted.

392. The pompous patient had annoyed everyone in the ward. The nurses were tired of his amorous advances at them, and the other patients had rapidly become irritated with his highly detailed boasts of his probably fictional conquests of numerous women.

One young nurse decided to teach the man a lesson.

'Now, sir, I want to take your temperature as the doctor instructed,' she explained. 'So I'll just close the screens around your bed and then you must take your pyjamas off.'

'Oh, ho, ho!' said the man, loudly. 'So you fancy a bit of slap and tickle with Mr Fantastic himself, eh? Fancy asking me to take my pyjamas off just to take my temperature! A likely story!'

'I'm serious,' insisted the nurse. 'The doctor has ordered a rectal temperature to be taken.'

'You mean, you want to stick the thermometer up my . . .'

'Yes,' replied the nurse hastily.

Soon the screens were in position around the man's bed, his pyjamas were removed, and the nurse carried out her plan.

'There, I'll have to leave the thermometer in position for a few minutes,' said the nurse, and left the enclosure around the bed.

For the next five minutes the ward was filled with muffled giggles and shrieks of laughter.

'What's all the noise?' asked the matron, entering the ward and noticing a lot of nurses and patients peering in through gaps in the screen around the man.

On entering the enclosure around the man's bed, the matron demanded of the man: 'What is the reason for this?'

'For what?' asked the man. 'The nurse is taking my temperature.'

'With *this*?' demanded the matron, taking a tulip out of the man's behind to the accompaniment of riotous laughter from the onlookers who were still peering in through the screens.

393. Hospital consultant: 'The woman in that bed is the love of my life.'

Matron: 'Then why haven't you married her?'

Hospital consultant: 'I can't afford to – she's a private patient.'

394. Nurse: 'Can I take your pulse?'

Patient: 'Why? Haven't you got one of your own?'

HOTELS

395. My hotel is so noisy I couldn't sleep at all last night.

I complained to the hotel manager and said I had specifically requested a quiet room. He said the *room* was quiet – it was the traffic outside, the lift next to it, and the people in all the other rooms that were noisy.

396. You can always tell if you're in a honeymoon hotel – all the couples start yawning at five in the afternoon.

397. 'Are the sheets clean?' asked a tourist at a small hotel in New York.

'Of course they're clean,' snapped the manager. 'I washed them only yesterday. If you don't believe me you can feel them – they're still damp.'

398. There were three conventions going on all at the same time and so when I arrived all the hotels were full.

'Surely you've had a cancellation?' I said to the receptionist at the biggest hotel. 'Surely there's a room for me somewhere?'

'I'm sorry,' replied the receptionist, 'but all the rooms are booked.'

'Isn't there perhaps another single man who is in a twin-bedded room and who might like to share the cost of the room?' I asked.

'Well,' said the receptionist, 'Mr Jones was forced to take a twin-bedded room three nights ago because no singles were available, and he did moan about the cost of it all, and he did share the room last night with another gentleman. But that gentleman found it most uncomfortable and quit.'

'Why?' I enquired.

'It would appear that Mr Jones has a snore that is louder than the noise of an electric saw or an aeroplane taking off.'

'That's all right,' I replied. 'I don't mind sharing with Mr Jones.'

So I was introduced to Mr Jones, he agreed to share his room with me, and I had a peaceful and pleasant night's sleep.

The next day the receptionist asked me: 'Did you sleep well?'

'Very well,' I replied.

The receptionist raised her eyebrows in slight astonishment, and asked: 'Did you use ear-plugs?'

'No,' I said. 'But when it was time to go to bed, I gave Mr Jones a sloppy wet kiss on his cheek, called him a gorgeous hunk of a man – and I think he spent the rest of the night sitting up wide awake and in panic, watching me.'

399. Hotel receptionist: 'Would you like a room with a private bath?'

Young man: 'That's all right, I'm not shy. I don't mind who sees me. The bath doesn't *have* to be private.'

400. The young man arrived late at night at a small hotel in a remote village in Scotland.

After a hot supper, the middle-aged owners of the hotel bid him good night, but warned him: 'Make sure you lock your bedroom door before going to sleep as our Stella walks in her sleep.'

The young man, with visions of a delicious young female named Stella sleep-walking into his room, made sure to leave his door open.

Two hours after falling asleep he was rudely awakened by a coarse tongue licking his face and a heavy weight on his chest and body. He opened his eyes to see Stella, the biggest sheep-dog he'd ever seen.

401. The new porter at a hotel in Mexico had been given

careful instructions as to how to behave with courtesy and efficiency.

'You should try and welcome each guest by name,' instructed the hotel manager.

'But how can I do that? How will I know their names?' asked the porter.

'Simple!' explained the manager. 'Each guest usually has his or her name written on their luggage.'

So the first couple to enter the hotel and be welcomed by the new porter were greeted: 'Welcome, Mr and Mrs Simulated Real Leather.'

402. My wife and I once stayed in an ancient hotel in an overseas resort. The corridors of the hotel had cobwebs and the swimming pool had green slime on it.

On the first morning of our stay we were woken by a pounding on the door.

I staggered out of bed, looked at my watch (it was 6 am) and opened the door.

'Sheets!' said a plump, middle-aged maid.

'What?' I asked.

'Sheets!' repeated the maid.

'We've got sheets,' I said. 'It's only six o'clock in the morning. Surely you don't change the sheets that early? We're staying in this hotel for another three days.'

'Sheets! Give me sheets,' insisted the maid, pushing past me and into the room, whereupon she started pulling the sheets off the bed.

'This is ridiculous,' said my wife. 'Can't you leave changing the sheets until later?'

'No time,' said the maid. 'Need sheets now for breakfast.'

'Why?' I asked.

'Must have sheets,' said the maid. 'Need to put on tables as tablecloths for breakfast.'

403. Hotel receptionist in Spain to Englishman: 'Are you a foreigner?'

Englishman: 'Certainly not! I'm British!'

404. A man arrived at a hotel in a large conference town.

'Do you have a room for the night?' he asked.

'I'm sorry,' said the receptionist, 'but we are fully booked. All the other hotels are probably full, too.'

'But surely,' said the man, 'you must be able to find some room somewhere? Suppose I was the Prime Minister in disguise – surely you'd find a room for him?'

'Yes, we would,' admitted the receptionist.

'Well,' said the man, 'as the Prime Minister isn't coming, please can I have his room?'

405. The weary traveller arrived at the small hotel in a strange town. 'Do you have a room for tonight?' he asked the hotel proprietor.

'Certainly, sir,' was the swift response. 'Would you like the expensive, luxurious room – or one much cheaper where you would have to make your own bed?'

'I'll take the cheap room,' said the traveller.

'Good!' said the hotel proprietor. 'I'll just go and fetch the wood, hammer and the nails and other materials for you to make the bed . . .'

HOUSEKEEPER

406. Mabel is the best housekeeper in the world. She's been divorced fifteen times – and each time she's kept the house.

HOUSES

407. I've stopped living in a house. I now live in a kennel. My kids made all my books dog-eared, my wife treats me like a dog, and all my work makes me dog-tired – so I might as well stay in the kennel.

408. I used to live in a house in Llanfighangel-Tal-y-llyn in

Wales – but I had to move because I couldn't spell the address.

HOUSE-WARMING PARTY

409. 'Would you like to come to my house-warming party on Friday?'

'I'd love to! What's the address?'

'Number six, Labrador Crescent. Just ring the bell with your elbow.'

'Why can't I ring it with my finger?'

'You're not coming empty-handed, are you?'

HUSBANDS

410. For twenty-two years my husband and I were happy – then we met and got married.

411. My husband used to be a professional violinist, but he had to give it up because it gave him a bad back. It was all the bending down to pick up the coins in the hat that did it . . .

412. The other day I saw my husband facing a mirror with his eyes closed. I asked him what he was doing and he said he was trying to see what he looked like when he was asleep.

413. My husband is a self-made man who loves his maker.

414. Janice: 'My husband tricked me into marrying him. Before we married he said he was a multi-millionaire.'

Berenice: 'He *is* a multi-millionaire, isn't he?'

Janice: 'Yes. But he also said he was eighty-one and in poor health – but I've just found out he's only eighty and in perfect condition.'

415. If my husband ever had any get-up-and-go it got up and went before I met him.

416. My husband is a very noisy eater. Last night we went to an exclusive, cosy little night club and when he drank his soup five couples got up to dance the cha-cha.

417. When I asked my husband why he parted his hair in the middle, he replied: 'It's so my head will be evenly balanced.'

418. Someone once asked me if I believed in clubs for promiscuous husbands. I said that poison was safer than using a club.

419. Joe got a letter from his wife today. It read: 'Dear Joe, I missed you yesterday. Please come home as soon as possible and let me have another shot.'

420. My husband is so pedantic, if you say to him 'How do you do?', he'll reply: 'Do what?'

421. My husband is so unpopular even his own shadow refuses to follow him around.

422. My husband is so short-sighted he can't get to sleep unless he counts elephants.

423. My husband believes so devoutly in reincarnation that in his Will he leaves everything to himself.

424. My husband is so thin and has such a gigantic nose and enormous ears that whenever he stands up in a restaurant people hang their coats and hats on him.

425. My husband keeps boasting to people at parties that he has more than a thousand people under him. So he does – he's a gardener in a cemetery.

426. My husband is so stupid that when I gave birth to triplets he wanted to know who the other two fathers were.

427. Last year the children and I had a lot of fun on holiday burying my husband in the sand on the beach. Next year we might go back and dig him up.

428. I know my husband's hair is all his own – I went with him when he made the final payment on his wig.

429. My husband is such a hypochondriac he refused to kiss me until I bought lipstick with penicillin in it.

430. You can always find my husband at a party, even if you've never met him before. All you have to do is find a situation where two people are talking – if one of them looks extremely bored, then it's my husband who's doing the talking.

431. I have a special soft spot for my husband – a large swamp in Africa.

432. I don't know what to make of my husband. I suppose if I was a cannibal I could make him into a casserole.

433. My sister has had five husbands – two of her own, and three married to friends.

434. I like to make my husband laugh on New Year's Day so I tell him jokes on Boxing Day.

435. My husband is a regular churchgoer – he never misses the Christmas Eve service.

436. My husband insists he's not bald – just that his hair is flesh-coloured.

437. My husband isn't exactly stupid – it's just that he's been educated beyond his intelligence.

438. My husband never gets a hangover – he's always drunk.

439. My husband wanted to be a tree surgeon when he was young – but he couldn't stand the sight of sap.

440. My husband has finally given up eating Smarties. He said it took too long to peel off the shells to get to the chocolate.

441. My husband has got such a long face that his barber charges him double for shaving it.

442. My husband always drinks with a friend – that way he's got someone to carry him home.

443. My husband keeps pining for his lost youth – he lost her to another boy at school.

444. My husband is so stupid, when I told him the car battery was dead he took it out and buried it.

445. When my husband told me that his pot belly had got a lot smaller, I told him it was only wishful shrinking.

446. My sister has just lost two hundred pounds of ugly fat – her husband left her.

447. Last year when I was on holiday in the USA I bought a lovely chair for my husband. Now all I've got to do is plug it in.

448. My husband isn't a hard drinker – he finds it very easy.

449. The only thing my husband ever achieved on his own is his moustache.

450. The reason my husband is so thin is because when he went to donate blood he forgot to say 'when'.

451. My husband has more chins than a Chinese telephone book.

452. People keep asking me if I mind that my husband chases after pretty young women. I tell them that it's a bit like dogs chasing after cars – they wouldn't know what to do if they caught one.

453. You can always tell when my husband has just told a joke at a party – the whole room goes deathly quiet.

454. My husband was such an ugly baby that his mother refused to push him in his pram – she pulled it.

455. I think I have the perfect husband. Pity I'm not married to him.

456. My husband can charm the birds out of the trees – vultures, crows, buzzards . . .

457. My husband says he is a man with many hidden talents. I suppose one day he might find one of them.

458. Fred came home early from work one day and found his wife in bed with the postman.

'What on earth do you think you're doing?' demanded Fred.

'I see what you mean,' said the postman to Fred's wife, continuing his exertions. 'He really is as stupid as you said he is, if he has to ask a question like that!'

I

INHERITED WEALTH

459. Claude was so wealthy that even the bags under his eyes had his initials on them.

460. The hereditary peer was boasting of his ancestors and generally acting in an arrogant and disdainful manner towards one of his fellow club members who was a self-made man.

Eventually, the man could stand the peer's attitude no longer and said, in a loud voice: 'From what you have been saying it would appear that the nobility of my family begins with me, whereas that of yours ended with your father.'

461. The extremely wealthy man (who had inherited his wealth) bought his son a slum. He wanted him to have everything he missed when he was a child.

462. The young man knew his aged aunt was extremely wealthy and dearly loved her poodles, so he visited her every day to take the dogs for walks in the hope of convincing his aunt that he was a suitable major beneficiary under her will.

A short time later the old lady died. She left him the poodles.

463. He's so wealthy he even bought a kid for his dog to play with.

INSURANCE

464. My wife is so silly she thinks a lump sum insurance policy only pays out if she gets lumps.

465. Insurance agent: 'Now, madam, this policy is a particularly good buy. Under it we pay up to five thousand pounds for broken arms or legs.'

Woman: 'But what do you do with them all?'

INVESTMENTS

466. Are stockbrokers so called because they sell you stock that makes you broke?

467. With so much uncertainty in the Stock Market, many investors are no longer bulls or bears – they're chickens or lemmings.

468. A friend once asked me for some investment advice. I asked him if he had any liquid assets. He said he did – three bottles of Scotch and a can of fizzy orange.

ITALY

469. I didn't have much trouble speaking Italian when I was on holiday in Italy – it was just that the Italians seemed to have trouble understanding it.

470. Edward was on holiday in Italy. While walking in a park he heard a female voice cry out in English: 'Get off, you beast! Get your filthy paws off me. Stop it!'

He rushed behind the hedge from where the voice had come, hoping to save a beautiful young girl from the unwelcome attentions of an Italian. Instead, he discovered a little old lady talking to her pet dog.

471. I was standing in a queue in a hamburger restaurant the other day when I overheard two girls talking. One girl was blonde, the other brunette.

'Did you manage to pick up any Italian when you were on holiday in Rome?' asked the blonde.

'Yes,' replied the brunette. 'Lots.'

'Let's hear some,' asked the blonde.

'Well,' replied the brunette, 'they all spoke almost perfect English.'

J

472. I once knew a Japanese gentleman who was so wealthy that he was considering buying himself what he called 'a place down South'. It was Australia.

473. It was an international television conference in the USA and the delegates were eating the farewell dinner of the conference.

A Japanese gentleman was sitting next to a delegate from Portland, Oregon. After the Japanese had finished his soup, the American asked him 'Likee soupee?' The Japanese gentleman nodded.

Throughout the meal, the American asked such questions as: 'Likee fishee?' and 'Likee drinkee?'

When the meal was finished, the chairman of the conference rose to his feet and introduced the Japanese gentleman as the guest speaker of the meeting.

The Oriental gentleman gave a witty, excellent speech on the future of broadcasting – speaking in English much better than anything the man from Oregon could manage.

After his speech, the Japanese gentleman returned to his seat and asked his American table companion: 'Likee speechee?'

JEWISH
474. A mohel opened a shop and displayed some plastic dustbins in the window. (A mohel is the person who carries out

the Jewish circumcision operation.)

Anyway, a man went into the shop and said: 'I'd like a plastic dustbin, please.'

The mohel replied: 'I'm afraid I don't sell them.'

'But you've got plastic dustbins in the window!' exclaimed the man.

'So?' shrugged the mohel, 'what would you have put in the window?'

JOBS

475. The young student was desperate for money and so in his vacation he decided to take a job in a local factory as it paid good wages.

'Now,' said the supervisor, 'your first job is to sweep the floor.'

'But I've got a BA degree,' said the student, 'and I'm currently studying for a masters in business administration.'

'Oh!' said the supervisor. 'In that case I'd better show you how to hold the broom.'

476. My wife is thinking of applying for a job as a telephone canvasser – she says she'll enjoy making little tents for telephones.

477. A friend of mine is very pleased with his wife. He thinks she's got a good part-time job with a London law firm, working two evenings each week. But all she told him was that to get money for a few extra luxuries, she would now be soliciting in Paddington.

478. My sister has a very responsible job. If anything goes wrong, she's responsible.

479. The best job for people who think they are paranoid is driving a taxi – then they really will always have people talking behind their backs.

480. My job is very secure – it's *me* they can do without.

481. When I left university I went for several job interviews. At the first interview I was turned down because I wasn't married. The personnel officer said that married men had much more experience of knowing how to cope if a boss shouted at them.

K

482. My wife was knitting the most peculiar garment last week. It had lots of strings at the top and a huge canopy. She said it was a parachute jumper.

483. 'Knock, knock.'
'Who's there?'
'Machiavelli.'
'Machiavelli who?'
'Machiavelli nice suit for seventy pounds.'

484. 'Knock, knock.'
'Who's there?'
'Luke.'
'Luke who?'
'Luke through the keyhole and you'll see who.'

485. 'Knock, knock.'
'Who's there?'
'Cook.'
'Cook who?'
'Oh, I didn't know it was Spring already.'

486. 'Knock, knock.'
'Who's there?'

'Ken.'
'Ken who?'
'Ken you please open the door and let me in.'

487. 'Knock, knock.'
'Who's there?'
'Hatch.'
'Hatch who?'
'Bless you!'

488. 'Knock, knock.'
'Who's there?'
'Who.'
'Who who?'
'Sorry, I don't talk to owls.'

489. 'Knock, knock.'
'Who's there?'
'Cows.'
'Cows who?'
'Cows don't go "who" they go "moo".'

490. 'Knock, knock.'
'Who's there?'
'Mary.'
'Mary who?'
'Mary Christmas and a Happy New Year.'

491. 'Knock, knock.'
'Who's there?'
'Howard.'
'Howard who?'
'Howard you like to stand here in the freezing cold and snow while some twit keeps asking "Who"?'

L

LAND

492. I once knew a man who was sold a plot of land at the North Pole. He thought it was the ideal place to grow frozen peas.

LAW

493. If it is the law of gravity that keeps us from falling off the Earth as it zooms around the Sun, what kept us on Earth before the law was passed?

494. 'Now,' said the prosecution counsel to the lady in the witness box, 'at the time of the car crash, what gear were you in?'

'Umm,' mused the lady, 'I think it was blue jeans and a tight white T-shirt.'

495. The complicated commercial lawsuit had dragged on for years and years.

'I've had enough of this,' said the managing director of one of the firms involved. 'Let's come to a compromise solution and settle out of court.'

'Impossible!' snorted the City solicitor. 'My firm is determined to fight your case right down to your last penny.'

496. 'Do you plead guilty or not guilty?'

'Don't I have any other choices?'

497. The solicitor died and went to the gates of Heaven where he was to be interviewed by St Peter to see if he should be let into Heaven or sent down to Hell.

'I don't know why I died so young,' said the solicitor. 'It doesn't seem fair. I'm only 35.'

'I know,' replied St Peter. 'But according to all the time you've billed your clients for, you're at least 208!'

498. The most difficult task a young lawyer ever had was the evening he spent trying to change a beautiful young lady's will.

499. Albert had just been found guilty of killing his very bossy and argumentative wife by pushing her out of the window of a room on the 29th floor of a hotel.

'This is a very serious offence,' said the judge. 'If your wife had fallen on someone there could have been a very nasty accident.'

500. The defendant in one court case said that at the time the crime was committed he was in hospital recovering from a vicious attack by a shark while swimming in the sea: he therefore had a water-bite alibi.

501. 'Members of the jury, have you reached your verdict?'

'Yes we have, your honour. We find the gorgeously sexy woman who stole the jewellery not guilty.'

502. 'Thank you for winning the case,' said the grateful client to her solicitor. He had won her £35,000 from the local council as she had tripped over an uneven paving slab on the pavement and injured her leg.

'It was a pleasure,' said the solicitor, handing the client his bill.

The client took the bill, then frowned: 'This bill is pretty steep. Is it right?'

'Of course,' replied the solicitor. 'It represents good value for all our time, care, experience, expertise and legal knowledge. If it wasn't for us, you wouldn't have won the case.'

'But your costs are almost half the damages,' replied the client. 'If it wasn't for me, you wouldn't have had a case.'

'But,' said the solicitor, 'anyone can trip over a paving slab.'

503. The criminal who stole a ton of rubber bands was given a long stretch.

504. Judge: 'Have you ever been up before me before?'

Defendant: 'I don't know, your honour. What time do you usually get up?'

505. The man had been arrested and charged with stealing five hundred cigars.

He consulted a solicitor for advice and was quoted a fee for defending him.

'I can't afford all that!' exclaimed the man. 'I'm completely innocent. Wouldn't you like some boxes of cigars instead of a cash fee?'

M

MAIDS

506. The Browns were a wealthy middle-aged couple who lived in a large house in the country. All went well for many years until a new maid arrived. She was extremely attractive. Within six months of her arrival, Mr Brown was starting to wake up every morning at 5 am instead of his usual 7.30 am.

'Where are you going?' Mrs Brown would ask, as her husband got out of bed and slipped on his dressing gown.

'Once awake, I can't get back to sleep,' Mr Brown replied, 'so I think I'll do some work in my study or walk around the garden. You don't need to get up – just go back to sleep. You know how deep sleep keeps you beautiful.'

Mrs Brown began to suspect that her husband was sneaking into the maid's room. What should she do?

It was soon to be the maid's parents' wedding anniversary, so one Thursday afternoon when Mr Brown was on a business trip to London, Mrs Brown suggested that the maid might like to pay a surprise visit to her parents.

'You can go now, if you like,' suggested Mrs Brown, 'and come back on Monday.'

'Thanks very much,' said the maid, 'it's most kind of you.' And she went off to pack for her trip.

Soon the maid had left the house. Mr Brown returned around 9 pm and, after watching TV for a bit, went to bed.

Promptly at 5 am, Mr Brown woke up and said he couldn't sleep any more and was going for a stroll around the garden.

As soon as her husband left the room, and she could hear him cleaning his teeth in the bathroom, Mrs Brown rushed to the maid's room and got into the maid's bed.

Mrs Brown had been lying in the dark for about five minutes when she heard the sash window of the room being slowly lifted and a man climbed in through the window.

Mrs Brown tensed herself in the darkness, but relaxed as the man made tender, passionate love to her. She was ecstatic. Why could her husband make such wonderful love to the maid and be so boring in bed with her?

'Darling,' whispered Mrs Brown, snuggling up to the man in bed, 'let's do it again.'

'Sorry, luv,' replied the man. Mrs Brown was aghast. It was not her husband's voice. 'No time for more now,' continued the man, 'but I can come back when I've finished the milk round.'

507. The gorgeous new maid had once been a gymnast in Romania. She was now trying to improve her English by working for Lord and Lady Spiffleburgson at their mansion in Dorset.

The maid had been with the Spiffleburgsons for only nine days and found many English habits rather strange. But she was determined to succeed as she desperately needed her salary to help support her family in Romania.

Thus it was that at a luncheon party at the mansion she walked in carefully carrying a large bowl of salad – but the guests were rather astonished that she was completely naked.

The gentlemen at the luncheon raised their eyebrows while secretly admiring her trim, lithe young body, while the ladies demurely tried to look away.

After the maid had placed the bowl of salad on the table and was leaving the room, Lady Spiffleburgson rose from her chair and accompanied the maid to the kitchen.

'My dear,' said her ladyship, 'why are you walking about naked?'

'I only obey your orders,' said the maid. 'I hear you say – you say several times – and you say it important for me to remember – I must serve salad without dressing.'

MARRIAGE

508. After we got married, I no longer had buttons missing from my shirts, and my clothes were no longer creased – my wife taught me how to sew and iron!

509. They were a well-matched couple as both of them were madly in love – she with herself, and he with himself.

510. My sister has just married for the fourth time. Her first husband was very wealthy. Her second husband was a theatrical producer and she wanted to be in one of his musicals. Her third husband liked donkeys – and she'd always wanted a donkey. And her current husband is Japanese and likes playing a game for two.

In fact, as far as husbands go, she's had one for the money, two for the show, three to get neddy, and four to play Go!

511. People keep saying that two can live as cheaply as one – but they never seem to finish the sentence: one *what*?

512. I married my husband because I thought he was rich. He said he owned a chain of newspapers.

The day after we married, he took me up to the attic of his mother's house and showed me what he did when he was a small boy at school – made a chain out of old newspapers.

513. The only reason Henrietta married Archibald is because he gave her an engagement ring, then she grew too fat to be able to get it off her finger and give it back to him.

514. I once knew a man who was so mean he spent years and years before he found his ideal wife – a woman born on 29th February so he would only have to buy her a birthday card every four years.

515. I can marry anyone I please. Trouble is, I haven't pleased anyone yet.

516. In many marriages there have been three rings: an engagement ring, a wedding ring – and suffering.

517. I was sitting on a train to London the other day when I overheard two young girls talking.

One girl said: 'Last night, Julian told me that he wanted to marry the cleverest, most beautiful girl in the world.'

'Oh,' replied the other girl, 'that's a pity. He's been your boyfriend for at least two years and now he says he's going to marry someone else.'

518. I married my wealthy husband because he said if I did he would be humbly grateful. Instead, he's been grumbly hateful.

519. For the whole of the first week of our marriage my wife went to bed every night wearing a white glove on her left hand, and a small white sock on her left foot. I thought this was rather odd, but didn't like to ask her about it until the second week I eventually plucked up courage.

'Darling,' said my demure bride, 'my mother said that if I wanted a long and happy marriage I should keep an air of mystery and never let you see me completely naked.'

MISERS

520. A miserly couple went to a restaurant in London and each of them ordered a steak.

The waiter was surprised to see the woman eating while the man merely looked at his plate without eating.

'Is there something wrong with your meal, sir?' asked the waiter.

'Oh, no!' replied the man. 'It's just that my wife is using the dentures first.'

521. An elderly miser was passing an undertakers when he noticed that they were having a 'cut price funeral' offer – so he went in and ordered one, then went home and committed suicide.

522. The rich, miserly lady discovered that her husband had died during the night. She wondered for a moment how to break the news to the servants. Then she rang her bell for the maid.

'Josephine,' said the thrifty lady, 'you need only boil *one* egg for breakfast.'

523. I once knew a man who was so miserly that he said he wouldn't want to buy a nuclear fall-out shelter now because it was cheaper to wait and get one second-hand.

524. The miser was so mean he even re-used the toilet paper.

525. The mean, wealthy lady was walking along a fashionable street in London when an unemployed young man begged her for money.

'I'm homeless, jobless, and I'm starving,' said the man. 'Please give me a few pounds for some soup.'

'You can get soup for less than that!' snapped the lady.

'I know,' said the young man, 'but I have to give the waiter a good tip.'

MOTHER-IN-LAW

526. My mother-in-law believes in free speech – particularly long-distance phone calls from our house.

527. For eleven years Duncan had put up with the fat, interfering old woman. Now he could stand it no longer.

'She's got to go,' he said to his wife. 'I can't stand your mother another minute!'

'My mother!' exclaimed Duncan's wife. 'I thought she was *your* mother!'

528. 'My mother-in-law has gone to the West Indies.'
'Jamaica?'
'No – she decided to go by herself.'

529. My mother-in-law is very spiteful. When she caught rabies she wrote down a list of people she wanted to bite.

530. They did things differently when my mother-in-law was a girl – otherwise they'd never have classified her as a girl.

531. 'My mother-in-law has gone to Indonesia.'
'Jakarta?'
'No – she went by plane.'

532. Fred: 'My mother-in-law arrived unexpectedly last night and since we were short of beds she had to sleep in the bath. But the stupid woman fell asleep and left the water running.
Tom: 'Did the bath overflow?'
Fred: 'No. My mother-in-law always sleeps with her mouth open.'

N

533. There I was on the beach on the far off paradise island when suddenly I was surrounded by a horde of shouting natives.

They moved in closer and closer and their shouts grew louder and their gestures grew more menacing and dramatic – so I had to give in and buy a cheap necklace and a gaudy T-shirt.

NEWS

534. The latest fashion news from Paris is that skirts will remain the same length as last year – but legs will be shorter.

535. I read in the newspaper today that a lot of people have recently been attacked at night and bitten just above the knee. Police are looking for a dwarf vampire.

536. Reports are just coming in about a woman photographer in Clapham who committed suicide by drinking a bottle of varnish. She left a note saying she did it because she wanted a glossy finish.

537. On Wednesday, three Irishmen hi-jacked a submarine, and then demanded a million pounds – and three parachutes.

538. On the business front, sales of tiaras increased enormously this afternoon – it was tiara boom today!

539. Five people broke out of prison last night by stealing a lorry load of senna pods. It is believed the criminals are still on the run.

540. A famous Australian jewel thief and homosexual was arrested in Sidney today.

541. I recently read a newspaper report of a survey that stated that one per cent of males liked women with fat thighs, six per cent preferred ladies with thin thighs – all the rest liked something in between.

542. The politician was on a fact-finding mission overseas and, when he arrived at the airport of one small country, he was greeted by a jostling crowd of newspaper reporters.

'Have you come to see the brothels?' asked one reporter.

The politician was temporarily stunned. Then, not wanting to offend, asked politely: 'Are there any brothels here?'

The next day there were banner headlines in the newspaper: VISITING POLITICIAN ASKS: 'ARE THERE ANY BROTHELS?'

NIGHTCLUBS

543. When the nightclub singer asked me if he sang in the right key, I said he sang more like a monkey.

544. My boyfriend takes me to all the best nightclubs – maybe one day they'll let us in.

545. I recently went to a nightclub where the dance floor was so crowded that when one of the dancers fainted it was half an hour before he could fall down.

O

OBITUARY COLUMNS

546. I always read the obituary columns every morning to see if I'm alive or dead.

547. My wife reads the obituary columns and thinks it very odd that people keep dying in alphabetical order.

OFFICE

548. Mavis, the office manager, was away on a training course when one of her colleagues enquired: 'What's happened to Mavis?'

Her secretary replied: 'She's abroad.'

'I know,' replied the colleague. 'But I want to know *where* she is, not *what* she is!'

549. Why do I have to work so much overtime at the office?

Because I owe, I owe, so off to work I go.

550. The new office boy was bitterly denying to his older colleague that he was a crawler: 'It's not true that I lick my boss's shoes every day – he's only in the office on Mondays and Thursdays.'

551. The young office girl was about to get married. Her colleagues made a collection and bought her a wedding present.

'Where shall we hide it until the boss can present it to her?'

asked one of her colleagues.

Just then the boss appeared. 'I heard that,' he said. 'Just put the present in a filing cabinet – she never seems capable of finding anything in there!'

552. 'Simpkins, how many people work in your office?'

'About half of them, sir.'

OLD AGE

553. The grand old man at the Home was celebrating his 112th birthday and the reporter from the local newspaper asked him: 'Tell, me, what do you think is the reason for your long life?'

The old man thought for a moment, then said: 'Well, I suppose it's because I was born such a long time ago.'

554. Every Saturday and Sunday my father goes to the Old Folks' Club. I don't know what exactly he does there – but he's got eight notches on his walking stick.

OPERATIONS

555. My wife recently asked me if it was possible for a six-year-old boy to perform heart transplant operations.

'Of course it's not possible,' I replied.

'Jonathan,' shouted my wife. 'Daddy says you can't possibly do the operations. So go and put the hearts back right now!'

P

556. I once went to an important business dinner party and was listening to an interesting conversation between two people at the far end of the table when the host (my boss) passed me a note.

I had forgotten to bring my spectacles, so I handed the note to the man on my right and asked him if he would be kind enough to read me the note as without my spectacles I find it difficult even to read newspaper headlines.

The man looked at the note and read: 'Please talk to the man on your right. He's a long-winded bore, full of his own self-importance and is rather stupid – but we're hoping to pick up a good order from his firm.'

557. Whenever I go to fancy dress parties I always go as Napoleon. That way, I can keep one hand on my wallet.

558. There I was at the office cocktail party. I'd spent a small fortune on a new suit and my wife had spent even more on her dress.

I wanted to impress my new boss, but my wife seemed to be letting me down. Every five minutes or so she would go over to the bar and get a drink and bring it back to where I was standing, and then rapidly drink it with her back to the bar.

By the time she had finished her seventh drink I noticed that my boss was watching her as she made her way back to the bar.

I wanted to go after my wife, but it was difficult to break off the conversation I was having with someone from the computer systems department. Out of the corner of my eye I could see my boss talking to my wife. He smiled. She smiled. He frowned. Then she walked back to me.

'Darling,' I said to my wife, when the computer systems man had moved on to buttonhole someone else, 'what did my boss say to you? Did he comment on all the drinks you've had? That won't do my career much good. He must think you've got a drink problem.'

'No he doesn't,' replied my wife. 'He certainly doesn't think I've got a drink problem. I'm *not* a liability to you, darling. I simply told him you just keep sending me to the bar to get more drinks for you.'

559. 'I say, old man,' said Clive to the host of the party, 'there's this rather delectable young chick whom I'm getting along really well with, if you know what I mean.' He winked, and continued: 'And I wondered if I might use your spare bedroom for a short while.'

'No, I don't mind,' replied the host, 'but what about your wife?'

'Oh, don't bother about her,' said Clive. 'I'll only be gone a short time and I'm sure she won't miss me.'

'I *know* she won't miss you,' stated the host, 'it's only five minutes ago that *she* borrowed the spare bedroom!'

560. It was a fancy dress party and the young girl said to the man: 'I'm supposed to be a turkey – what are you?'

'Sage and onions,' he replied.

PASSPORTS

561. When my husband complained that his new passport photo didn't do him justice, I told him that he didn't really want justice – he needed mercy.

562. When you look just like your passport photo you know you're really too sick to travel.

PERSONNEL MANAGER

563. 'What can you do?' asked the Personnel Manager.

'Lots,' replied the young man. 'I can play golf, talk in a public school accent, make boring speeches, have affairs with secretaries without my wife finding out, go to sleep in the back of a Rolls Royce, and generally get publicity for working as hard as possible while in reality doing nothing at all.'

'Excellent,' said the Personnel Manager. 'You can start tomorrow as Managing Director.'

PETS

564. I once knew a rather ridiculous man who named his pet zebra 'Spot'.

PHILOSOPHY

565. Philosophy of a skunk: I stink, therefore I am.

PICNIC

566. For the summer Saturday outing to the park, the little girl put a small furry animal into a wicker basket – it was her picnic hamster.

PIES

567. 'Dad, can pies fly?'

'No, of course not, son.'

'But mum insists that there are two magpies flying around the garden.'

PIGEON RACING

568. One of my cousins says he wants to take up pigeon racing – but I'm sure he'll never win against them unless he learns how to fly.

PLANE TRAVEL

569. I was on a plane the other day, sitting next to an elderly woman who was on her first flight.

Just before take-off, the stewardess came round with some boiled sweets and explained to the elderly woman that the sweets would help to reduce the pressure in her ears.

Half an hour after take-off, the elderly woman asked the stewardess if it was now all right to take the sweets out of her ears.

570. I knew it was going to be a plane flight with a difference when a naked man rushed down the aisle shouting: 'This is your captain streaking . . .'

571. I was on a plane from Moscow to New York when a man got up from a seat a few rows behind me and began to walk down the aisle towards the toilets and the front of the plane.

He looked rather menacing. He was wearing scruffy jeans and a bulky leather jacket which was firmly zipped up. His hands were in his jacket pockets.

Suddenly, he stopped. He looked to where I was sitting and said: 'Hijack.'

I was terrified. He said the word again, even louder: 'Hijack!'

The man sitting next to me put down the copy of *The Astute Private Investor*, an excellent book which he had been reading. He looked up at the man in the aisle and said: 'Hi George. How are you? I didn't know you were on this plane, too.'

572. As the plane flew over the sea I saw something large, black and hairy in the water. It was an oil wig.

PLUMBERS

573. I think my three young sons are going to be plumbers when they grow up – they never come when they're called.

POET

574. The poet had been boring everyone at the party by droning on and on about his various sources of inspiration and how he was trying to write a poem composed of distichs in elegiac form.

Towards the end of the party he approached a sweet young girl and said: 'You know, I'm currently collecting some of my better poems for an anthology to be published post-humously.'

'Oh good!' said the girl, with true feeling. 'I shall look forward to it!'

575. A friend of mine is a poet and he's almost starving. He says that rhyme doesn't pay.

POLICE

576. The pretty young girl coming home by car late at night after visiting her boyfriend's house was stopped by a policeman and asked to take the breath test.

The girl blew into the breathalyzer and it instantly changed colour.

'Hmm,' said the policeman. 'You've had a stiff one tonight miss.'

'My God!' exclaimed the girl. 'Does that show, too?'

577. Amanda Guv dyed her hair blonde when she became a policewoman so that when she made an arrest people could genuinely say: 'It's a fair cop, Guv.'

578. The police were rather suspicious when Bo Peep said she had lost her sheep. She had a crook with her.

579. Detective's assistant: 'Sir, I have found a box of vestas with your name on it.'

Detective: 'Ah! So at last I have met my match.'

POLITICS

580. Why is it that lunatics and criminals are not allowed to vote – but you *are* allowed to vote for *them*?

581. I understand that they are going to erect a huge statue in Trafalgar Square of ——— [insert the name of your own least favourite politician]. They are doing it so the pigeons can express the views of us all.

582. Someone once said that politicians stand for whatever the people will fall for.

583. A relative of mine, Andrew, once went canvassing on behalf of the Labour Party.

The first door he knocked on was opened by a formidable-looking lady with a piercing voice. Seeing Andrew's Labour rosette, the lady launched into a tirade of abuse about the Labour Party, its leaders, MPs, and supporters. 'Utter trash, the lot of them!' she snorted. 'And their policies – if they can ever find them and follow them – stink. Absolute garbage!'

The lady was about to shut the door when Andrew said, rather meekly: 'Does that mean you won't be voting Labour?'

584. Did you hear about the Conservative MP who, when drunk, revealed such terrifying views to a journalist that he was dumped by his local party organization, ostracized by his former friends, and had to go and live in Australia?

He is now a far off terror Tory.

585. When a politician says he's 100% behind you, he usually forgets to mention he's also holding a knife.

POLO

586. The reason I don't play polo is because I think it must be incredibly difficult to ride a horse while using a stick to hit little mints.

POST OFFICE

587. The little old lady went to the post office and handed over the counter a large parcel, on which she'd written 'Fragile' numerous times and in large letters.

Counter clerk: 'Is there anything breakable in this parcel?'

Little old lady: 'Of course not! "Fragile" simply means unbreakable in Latvian.'

PRESS REVIEWS

588. 'We hope the author will soon be needing our services.' – *The Coffin Makers' Gazette.*

589. 'The writer of this book is a genius. By the way, I must thank him for such a fantastic weekend at his cottage in the country. This, of course, in no way influenced my opinion of his work.' – *A Female Critic*.

590. 'This book is brilliant.' – *Daily Liar*.

591. He is a man who recognises true genius (he gave my novel a good review) and his latest book is excellent. – *A Back-Scratcher*.

592. 'He is certainly one of our best writers and will surely become as famous as William Shakespeare – the William Shakespeare of 112 Railway Arches, Neasden, Alaska.' – *Anony Mouse*.

PRIVATE DETECTIVE

593. I used to be a private detective. I once had to follow a woman from London to Bournemouth, where she gave me the slip.

Another time I managed to follow her to Newcastle, where she again gave me the slip.

Then I followed her to London where she gave me the slip.

Then I got lucky. When I followed her to York she not only gave me the slip – but her bra and panties, too!

PROMOTION
594. When Simpkins-Smutterwhite was promoted above me – even though I had been with the company for much longer, had more experience and worked much harder than he did – I was not upset. I went straight up to him and said: 'Congratulations! Let me shake you by the throat.'

PROVERBS
595. People who cough loudly never go to the doctor – they go to the cinema.

596. The more you understand the less you realize you know.

597. Laugh and the world laughs with you: weep and you sleep alone.

598. Every woman worries about the future until she has acquired a husband, whereas men never worry about the future until they get a wife.

599. Success doesn't always go to the head – more often it goes to the mouth.

600. Anyone who boasts about his ancestors is admitting that his family is better dead than alive.

601. The less people know, the more stubbornly they know it.

602. The first sign of old age is when you still chase girls but can't remember why.

603. If at first you don't succeed you're just like 99.99 per cent of the population.

604. You can always tell when politicians are lying – their lips move.

605. The best distance between two points is cleavage.

606. If it wasn't for venetian blinds it would be curtains for all of us.

607. Men who call women 'birds' should remember that birds pick up worms.

608. A hypochondriac's life is a bed of neuroses.

609. People who sleep like babies never have any.

610. One of the first signs of getting old is when your head makes dates your body can't keep.

611. The only way in Britain to make money go further is to post it overseas.

612. Absence makes the heart go wander.

613. Never try to make love in a field of corn. It goes against the grain.

PSYCHIATRIST

614. The young woman was visiting the male psychiatrist for the first time, and he decided to test her reactions to different pictures.

First, he held up a card on which had been drawn two circles that almost touched.

'What does this make you think of?' asked the psychiatrist.

'Two fat people about to make love,' replied the young woman.

The psychiatrist showed the woman a picture of two wavy lines.

'That looks like the sand on the beach after two people have made passionate love for hours – or maybe it's a waterbed rocking in motion to some lovers in action.'

'Hmm,' said the psychiatrist, leaning back in his chair. 'You seem to be overly pre-occupied with sex.'

'How dare you!' snapped the woman. 'It was *you* that showed me the sexy pictures.'

615. When Harry told his girlfriend he was seeing a psychiatrist, she admitted that she was seeing her boss, the local garage mechanic and a rather handsome window cleaner.

Q

616. What do you get if you cross a chicken with a clock?
An alarm cluck.

617. What do you call a plump pet cat that has eaten a duck?
A duck-filled fatty puss.

618. How can you stop milk from turning sour?
Leave it in the cow.

619. What did the policeman say to his stomach?
I've got you under a vest.

620. What tuba cannot be played?
A tuba toothpaste.

621. What walks about saying: 'Ouch, ouch, ouch, ouch, ouch, ouch, ouch, ouch'?
An octopus wearing shoes that are too tight.

622. Who was old, had a lot of children, and was rather sticky?
The Old Woman Who Lived In The Glue.

623. What did the skunk do in church?
It sat in a phew.

624. What is small, round, smells and giggles?
A tickled onion.

625. Where was the Declaration of Independence signed?
At the bottom.

626. What says 'Oom, oom'?
A backward cow.

627. What game do mice like to play?
Hide and squeak.

628. What is the difference between a coyote and a flea?
One howls on the prairie, while the other prowls on the hairy.

629. What do you get if you cross a pig with an evergreen tree that has cones?
A porker-pine.

630. Why was the young glow worm a bit sad?
Because it had glowing pains.

631. What game do horses like to play?
Stable tennis.

632. What do you use for measuring the noise a dog makes?
A barking meter.

633. Why did the baby pig eat so much food?
So it could make a hog of itself.

634. What was the largest moth in the world?
A mam-moth.

635. Where do cows go for outings?
To the moo-vies.

636. Where do intelligent cows like to visit on their holidays?
Moo-seums.

637. What do you do when your nose goes on strike?
Picket.

638. What is furry, crunchy, and makes a noise when you pour milk on it?
Mice crispies.

639. What is the favourite food of hedgehogs?
Prickled onions.

640. Where do very young fish go to be educated?
Plaice school.

641. What do young witches like best in school?
Spelling lessons.

642. What do you get if a witch gets flu?
Cold spells.

643. What is the difference between an oak tree and a very tight shoe?
One makes acorns – the other makes corns ache.

644. What slithers along the ground and works for the Government?
A civil serpent.

645. What ring can never be round?
A boxing ring.

646. Where did the major-general keep his armies?
Up his sleevies.

647. What game do cows play at parties?
Moo-sical chairs.

648. Why do storks only lift one leg?
Because if they lifted the other leg they would fall over.

649. Where does Friday come before Tuesday?
In a dictionary.

650. Why can't a bicycle stand up?
Because it's two-tyred.

651. What do you call a very large animal which keeps taking pills?
A hippo-chondriac.

652. What are the largest ants in the world?
Gi-ants and eleph-ants.

653. Where do underwater creatures go when their teeth hurt?
To a dental sturgeon.

654. What is very big and says, 'Fum, Fo, Fi, Fee?'
A backward giant.

655. How did the otters manage to travel at fifty miles per hour on the motorway?
By travelling in an otter-mobile.

656. Why are rivers lazy?
Because they seldom leave their beds.

657. Why do bees have sticky hair?
Because they use honey combs.

658. Which side of a sheep has the most wool?
The outside.

659. How can you easily make a witch itch?
Remove the 'w'.

660. How do you stop toadstools appearing in your garden?
Give the toads some sofas instead.

661. What fish races through the water at ninety miles an hour?
A motor pike.

662. Why did the singer gargle with soup?
Because she was a souprano.

663. What tiles are the most difficult to fix to the bathroom wall?
Reptiles.

664. What do rich turtles wear?
People-necked sweaters.

665. What happens to plants left in the maths teacher's room?
They grow square roots.

666. How do you start a flea race?
One, two, flea, go!

667. What is in Paris, is very tall, and wobbles?
The Trifle Tower.

668. What did the vampire doctor shout out in his waiting room?
'Necks please!'

669. What do you call a witch's husband when he's travelling on her broomstick?
A flying sorcerer.

670. What is the last thing you take off before going to bed?
Your feet off the floor.

671. Where do you take a sick horse?
To a horsepital.

672. What do policeman eat for tea?
Truncheon meat.

673. What was the first thing Henry III did on coming to the throne?
He sat down.

674. What do you call a man who breaks into a house and steals ham?
A ham burglar.

675. What is the favourite flower of a pet frog?
A croakus.

676. What two letters of the alphabet hurt teeth?
D.K.

677. Who are the two largest females in the USA?
Mrs Sippi and Miss Ouri.

678. What do elves and pixies have to do when they come home from school?
Gnomework.

679. What clothes does a house wear?
A dress.

680. What do you get when you cross some grass seed with a cow?
A lawn moo-er.

681. What do you call a lot of girls waiting in line to buy some dolls with yellow-blonde hair?
A Barbie-queue.

682. Have you heard the story about the giant gate?
You'll never get over it.

R

RAINY DAY

683. Years ago, Mr Smith gave his wife a large strong box and encouraged her to put something away for a rainy day. When she died, Mr Smith opened the box – and found seven umbrellas, six pairs of wellington boots and fourteen raincoats.

RATS

684. 'Did you hear about Adam?' asked the brown rat.

'No. What happened?' said the black rat.

'He was feeling rather depressed and flushed himself down the toilet.'

'Oh!' said the black rat. 'He committed sewer-cide.'

RELATIVES

685. The quickest way to find long-lost relatives is for the news to leak out that you have won a major lottery jackpot.

RELIGIOUS

686. Rabbi Cohen and Father O'Connor were at a party when they were each offered a ham sandwich.

Rabbi Cohen declined the sandwich, and the Catholic priest chided him: 'Come, come, rabbi – when are you going to become liberal enough to eat ham?'

The rabbi smiled and replied: 'At your wedding, Father O'Connor.'

687. Two drunks, Fred and Bill, were walking along the road when Fred said: 'Hey! Ishn't that man over th-there the Archbishop of Canterbury?'

'No,' replied Bill. 'It can't be.'

'It ish!' said Fred. 'I'll go over and ask him.'

Fred staggered over to the man and said: 'Ex . . . excuse me. But are you the . . . the Archbishop of Canterbury?'

'Get lost, you pathetic drunken creep,' replied the man, 'or I'll smash your face in!'

Fred staggered back to Bill.

'Was it the Archbish?' asked Bill.

'I don't know,' replied Fred. 'The st . . . stupid man refused to answer my question.'

688. The rabbi and the priest lived next door to each other and bought new cars almost exactly at the same time.

Looking out of his window, the rabbi saw the priest with a small bowl of water sprinkling the contents over the car and blessing it.

Not to be outdone, the rabbi got a hacksaw and cut half an inch off the exhaust pipe of his own car.

689. Cynthia: 'What do you think of the new clergyman?'

Janice: 'Very good. I didn't know much about sin until he came.'

690. The vicar asked the young man: 'Are you ever troubled by erotic thoughts about the opposite sex?'

'No,' replied the young man, 'I rather like the thoughts. They're no trouble.'

691. If Moses had been a lawyer, there wouldn't have been Ten Commandments. Instead there would have been many thousands of commandments, each with numerous clauses and sub-clauses.

692. Monica had decided to become a nun and remain a nun for the rest of her life. But after two years in the nunnery she kept having romantic thoughts about the handsome young gardener.

Eventually, one thing led to another, and immediately after the incident in the potting shed, Monica felt she had to go to the Mother Superior to confess her sin.

'I will sack the gardener immediately,' said the Mother Superior. 'And you can go and drink half a pint of vinegar while I ponder your future.'

'Vinegar!' exclaimed Monica. 'Why vinegar?'

'Because,' said the Mother Superior, 'it seems necessary to get rid of that glowing smile that's still on your face.'

693. Jewish men are very optimistic. The proof of this is that they all have a bit cut off before they know how long it's going to be.

RESTAURANTS

694. Customer: 'Why is this chop so terribly tough?'

Waiter: 'Because, sir, it's a karate chop.'

695. I was once invited by a business colleague for a meal in an expensive restaurant while on a sales trip to Germany.

The whole restaurant was decorated with the stuffed heads of animals. We had to sit next to a wall on which was hung the huge head of a rhinoceros.

'My goodness!' I said to the waiter. 'That rhino looks fierce.'

'It was,' admitted the waiter. 'It killed my father.'

'I'm sorry to hear that,' I said. 'Did it happen on safari in Africa?'

'No,' said the waiter. 'It happened here in Germany. My

father was sitting in a chair underneath the rhino head when it dropped off the wall and hit him.'

696. Customer: 'Excuse me, but how long have you been working here?'
  Waitress: 'About three months, sir.'
  Customer: 'Oh. Then it couldn't have been you who took my order.'

697. 'Waiter! There's a fly in my soup.'
  'Would you prefer it to be served separately?'

698. 'Waiter! There's a fly in my soup.'
  'If you throw it a pea it'll play water polo.'

699. 'Waiter! There's a fly in my soup.'
  'No sir, that's the chef. The last customer was a witch doctor.'

700. 'Waiter! There's a fly in my soup.'
  'If you leave it there the goldfish will eat it.'

701. 'Waiter! There's a fly in my soup.'
  'I know, sir! It's fly soup.'

702. 'Waiter! There's a fly in my soup.'
  'Oh, dear, it must have committed insecticide.'

703. 'Waiter! There's a fly in my soup.'
  'I'm sorry, sir, the dog must have missed it.'

704. 'Waiter! There's a fly in my soup.'
  'That's the meat, sir.'

705. 'Waiter! There's a fly in my soup.'
  'It's the rotting meat that attracts them, sir.'

706. 'Waiter! How dare you splash soup on my trousers!'
  'I'm sorry, sir, but now you've got soup in your fly.'

707. 'Waiter! Please bring me a coffee without cream.'

'I'm very sorry, madam, but we've run out of cream. Would you like it without milk instead?'

708. Times were hard. Keith was sacked from his office job and went to work as a waiter in a restaurant. Soon after, one of his fellow redundant office workers came in.

'Fancy seeing *you* working in a place like *this*,' scoffed the man.

'So?' replied Keith. 'Fancy *you* being reduced to having to eat in a dump like this!'

709. David: 'I know this lovely little restaurant where we can eat dirt cheap.'

Barbara: 'Cheap or not, I don't fancy eating dirt.'

710. When the waiter asked my boyfriend if he wanted a fingerbowl he replied: 'No thank you, I don't eat fingers.'

711. My hotel is quite nice. At dinner in the restaurant last night there was a young girl at a table next to mine. She had chicken breasts and frog's legs – but her face was beautiful.

712. An American tourist, visiting England, had just enjoyed a delicious dinner in a Winchester restaurant.

'Would you like coffee, sir?' inquired a waiter.

'Certainly,' replied the American

'Cream or milk?'

'Neither,' said the American, firmly. 'Just give me what I'm used to back home: a pasteurized blend of water, corn syrup solids, vegetable oil, sodium caseinate, carrageenan, guargum, disodium phosphate, polysorbate 60, sorbitan monostearate, potassium sorbate and artificial colour.'

713. Customer: 'Have you got asparagus?'

Waiter: 'No, we don't serve sparrows and my name is *not* Gus.'

714. Man: 'Can I have a table for dinner?'

Waiter: 'Certainly, sir. Do you want the table fried, boiled, steamed or roasted?'

715. Waiter: 'What would you like, sir?'

Customer: 'Steak and chips.'

Waiter: 'Would you like anything with it, sir?'

Customer: 'If it's like the last one I ate here, then bring me a hammer and chisel.'

716. Waiter: 'Would you like something to eat?'

Customer who has waited forty-five minutes for service: 'No, thank you – I don't want to waste my lunch hour.'

RETIREMENT

717. The couple had just reached retirement age, but Mr Robinson was a very worried man.

'We don't really have enough to live on,' he confessed to his wife. 'Sure, our pension is enough to survive on – but we lack sufficient savings to give us a few extra pleasures like the occasional evening at the cinema or a decent holiday once a year.'

'Don't worry,' replied Mrs Robinson. 'I've managed to save quite a bit.'

'However did you manage that?'

'Well,' said Mrs Robinson, a bit shyly, 'every time you made love to me over these past thirty years I've taken a modest amount out of the housekeeping money and put it in my own bank account.'

'But why did you keep it a secret all these years?' demanded Mr Robinson. 'If I'd known about it I'd have given you all my business.'

ROMANCE

718. Bill can read his girlfriend like a book – in bed.

719. 1st girl: 'What would you give a man who has everything?'
   2nd girl: 'Encouragement.'

720. Girl: 'I'll pour the drinks, dear. What will you have – gin and platonic?'
   Young man: 'I was hoping for whisky and sofa.'

721. Paul: 'Is it true you proposed to that awful Gruntswick woman at the party last night?'
   David: 'Unfortunately, yes.'
   Paul: 'And she accepted your proposal. But didn't you only meet her at the party?'
   David: 'Yes. But after five or six dances together I couldn't think of anything else to talk about.'

722. When I told my cousin that I'd fixed him up with a date with an attractive librarian he said: 'What part of Libraria does she come from?'

723. Catherine snuggled up to her boyfriend, Robert, and whispered: 'Darling, now that you want us to get engaged, will you give me a ring?'
   Robert smiled lovingly at Catherine and replied: 'Certainly! What's your phone number?'

724. A friend of mine recently introduced me to his new girlfriend and said he was madly in love with her and was going to marry her in a few days' time.
   I recognized her as the notorious woman who had slept with half the men in Basingstoke. I managed to get my friend into a quiet corner and broke this news to him. But he just shrugged his shoulders and said: 'So? Basingstoke's not very big.'

725. My friend, Freda, has been writing to a male penfriend for eighteen months. He lives two hundred miles away.
   Gradually their letters grew more and more romantic, until eventually they felt they had to meet each other.

'Unfortunately,' wrote the man, 'I am seven feet tall, have an enormous nose, and my ears stick out.'

'Don't worrry,' wrote back Freda. 'Your letters showed me your true self. But when you arrive at Paddington Station please hold a carnation in your left hand so that I can recognize you.'

726. In romance, opposites frequently attract. That is why poor young girls are often attracted to rich old men.

727. I recently overheard two women talking on a train. One said to the other: 'I hear you've broken up with John. But only last week you told me it was love at first sight.'

'I know,' came the reply, 'it *was* love at first sight. But when I saw him for the second time I went off him.'

728. 'My dearest, sweetest, beautiful darling! Will you love me always?'

'Of course, darling. Which way do you want to try first?'

729. My first job was as a clerical officer and I really fancied a young typist. Eventually I plucked up enough courage and asked her: 'Could I have a date?'

'Certainly,' she replied. 'How about 1066?'

730. 'It's not fair! I've proposed to two boyfriends without avail.'

'Maybe next time you should wear a veil?'

731. 'Where have I seen your beautiful face before?'

'I don't know – it's always been between my ears.'

732. The couple were on a pre-honeymoon cruise when suddenly a storm blew up and their ship was smashed to pieces by the powerful waves.

Clinging to a plank of wood, the couple managed to survive in the sea for two days without food or water.

On the third day, the man began to pray even more frantically than before: 'Oh, dear Lord, please save us. Please – we beg you to spare our lives and make us safe and end our misery in this cruel sea. Please – if you save us I promise to give up the sins of gambling, smoking, swearing, drinking, and I will refrain from . . .'

He was interrupted by his girlfriend, who said: 'Better stop there – I think we're approaching land!'

733. An old gentleman asked the pretty girl if she wanted to come up to his room to help him write his will.

734. 'I love you much, much more than anyone else in the whole wide world.'

'You mean, you've had them all, too?'

735. Young girl: 'Darling, will you love me when I get old?'

Young man: 'Of course I'll love you. Our love will grow stronger with each passing hour. Our love will endure throughout eternity. But you won't be looking like your mother, will you?'

736. David and Debbie both worked in the same office in Hong Kong, and both of them were Chinese.

For more than six months David had admired Debbie from a distance, never managing to pluck up sufficient courage to ask her for a date, but all the time his passion for her grew stronger and stronger.

At last the great day came when he somehow managed to scrawl a note to her asking if she'd like to have dinner at a restaurant with him.

'I'd love dinner with you,' she replied, coming over to his desk in their open-plan office to tell him so in person, and making him blush with pleasure.

That evening in the restaurant he asked her what she would like to eat, and she studied the menu carefully, then said, 'I'll have shark's fin soup, please. And Peking duck with dumplings, some suckling pig, steamed fish, and then some fresh lychees.'

David was horrified, as he'd been mentally calculating the enormous cost of all this food – the most expensive items on the menu and more suitable for a wedding feast than for a dinner for two.

'D . . . D . . . do you eat like this at home?' he stammered, his face blushing red again.

'No,' replied Debbie. 'But then, no one at home desperately wants to go to bed with me.'

737. Samantha to her sister: 'My boyfriend has finally persuaded me to say "yes".'

'Fantastic!' replied Dolly. 'Congratulations. When will the wedding be?'

'Wedding? Who said anything about a wedding?'

738. Ethel: 'Dearest, will you still love me when my hair has all gone grey?'

Richard: 'Of course, dear. If I loved you when your hair was blonde then brunette then black then red – why should grey make any difference?'

739. I once knew a man who was very shy with women. He was much too meek to approach them, and wondered what he could do to get women to approach him instead. Then he had a bright idea and changed his name to Right as he had read that millions of women were searching for, and wanted to meet, Mr Right.

740. 'I'll give you just fifteen minutes to stop doing that . . .'

741. When I first went out with my girlfriend she made me lay all my cards on the table – Barclaycard, American Express . . .

742. The beautiful young girl was walking along the street when a young man walked up beside her and said: 'Hello, beautiful! Haven't we met somewhere before?'

The girl gave him a frosty stare and continued walking.

'Huh!' snorted the young man. 'Now I realize my mistake – I thought you were my mother.'

'That's impossible,' retorted the girl, 'I'm married.'

743. 'That man's annoying me.'

'Why? He's not even looking at you.'

'I know. *That's* what's annoying me!'

744. Mavis fell in love with her boyfriend at second sight – the first time she didn't know he had any money.

745. It had been a very enjoyable party and Jake, a young man with a Texan drawl, appeared to get on very well with a pretty young English girl named Sally – although both had met each other for the first time at the party.

'Can I see you home?' inquired Jake.

Sally reached into her handbag and produced a photograph of her house.

746. Peter received the following letter from his girlfriend:
'Darling Peter,

I'm so sorry I quarrelled with you and called off our wedding. I'm terribly, terribly sorry for all the hateful and spiteful things I said about you and do hope you will forgive me. Whatever you want of me I shall try to give – and do hope you will give me one more chance. I know I said I was leaving you for Tony, saying he was a much better man than you, but I never honestly meant it. Tony means nothing to me. You are the only one in my heart. You, Peter, are all that I desire. Please forgive me and take me back,

Your ever-loving Janice.

P.S.: May I take this opportunity to congratulate you on winning such a large amount on the Lottery.

747. The young girl was snuggling up to the young man on the sofa and said: 'Would you like to see my birthmark?'

'Yes,' replied the young man. 'How long have you had it?'

748. Sally and Sarah were talking about the wonderful party they had just attended.

'That George was really hunky,' said Sally.

'I know,' sighed Sarah.

'He and I got on really well,' said Sally. 'He wants to see me again and asked for my phone number.'

'Did you give it to him?' asked Sarah.

'I told him my number was in the phone book.'

'Does he know your name?' asked Sarah.

'I told him that was in the phone book, too. I can't wait until he phones . . .'

749. Some young women are music lovers – and others can do it without.

750. The young man asked the beautiful young girl to marry him, pointing out that his father was 103 years old and that he was heir to his father's substantial fortune.

The girl asked the young man for time to consider his offer and, two weeks later, she became his step-mother.

751. 'Will you kiss me?'

'But I have scruples.'

'That's all right. I've been vaccinated.'

752. Young girl: 'Darling, do you think I should wear my short green Chinese silk dress or my long fawn woollen dress tonight?'

Young man: 'I don't mind what you wear, dearest. You know I'll love you through thick or thin.'

753. 'How was your first date with John?'

'Oh, it was all right until after dinner. But on the way home he stopped the car in a lonely lane and started kissing me and generally distracting my attention. He then started feeling my bra and around my panties – but I fooled him. I'd hidden my money in my shoe . . .'

754. My girlfriend told me last night that she really loved me. But I think it's only puppy love as she was panting, licking my face, and rubbing me behind the ears at the time.

755. It was in a nudist camp and the beautiful young woman walked over to the young man.

'Pleased to meet you,' said the man.

The girl looked down, blushed, and said: 'I can see you are.'

756. Adrian: 'Why do all the men find Victoria so attractive?'

Simon: 'Because of her speech impediment.'

Adrian: 'Her speech impediment?'

Simon: 'Yes. She can't say "no".'

757. Cuthbert: 'Darling, if we get married do you think you will be able to live on my income?'

Ethel: 'Of course, darling. But what are *you* going to live on?'

758. My girlfriend rejected me because she said she liked the little things in life – a little house in the country, a little yacht, a little multi-millionaire . . .

759. A man of thirty was talking to his girlfriend. 'I've been asked to get married hundreds of times,' he said.

'Oh!' replied his girlfriend, rather astonished. 'Who by?'

'My parents,' he replied.

760. After going into Hazel Wood with his girlfriend, a disappointed Fred came out and wrote under the sign which said 'Hazel Wood' the words: 'but Janice wouldn't.'

761. 'Sir, I'd very much like to marry your daughter,' said young Wilkins, a junior clerk in the Company in which his prospective bride's father was the Personnel Officer.

'I see,' replied the man. 'Write out your qualifications, name, address and any other details you think appropriate and leave it with me. If no other suitable applicants turn up then I'll ask you to come for a further interview.'

762. Man: 'What would I have to give you to get a little kiss?'
Girl: 'Chloroform.'

763. John saw a beautiful young girl walking along the beach, dressed in an extremely tight pair of denim shorts which emphasized every movement of her walk.

Being a daring sort of fellow, he went up to the young girl and said: 'I'm sorry to trouble you – but I'm fascinated about your shorts. How can anyone possibly manage to get inside such a tight garment?'

The beautiful young girl smiled and replied: 'You can start by asking me out to dinner.'

764. 'Whisper those three little words that will make me walk on air.'

'Go hang yourself.'

765. Mabel and Arthur had been living together for thirty-five years as man and wife.

One day Mabel was reading a romantic women's magazine when she suddenly looked up at Arthur and said: 'Why don't we get married?'

'Don't be crazy,' replied Arthur. 'Who would want to marry us at our time of life?'

766. Overheard in a dimly lit nightclub: 'Do you know the difference between sex and conversation?'

'No.'

'Then why not come back to my apartment and lie down while I talk to you?'

767. With so many romantics they must be on Crowd Nine.

768. 'Would you agree to come out with me tonight?'
'I'm sorry, but I never go out with perfect strangers.'
'Who said I was perfect?'

769. Dennis knew he was really getting places with his girlfriend, Carol, when she invited him around to her parents' house, saying: 'We can have a great time together, I'm sure, as my parents are going to a concert and will be out the whole evening.'

Thus, on the great day he stopped in at a chemist's shop on his way to his girlfriend's house. The chemist was such a friendly man that Dennis found himself confiding to him about how beautiful Carol was and how he hoped she would appreciate his thoughtfulness in coming prepared with some contraceptives.

When Dennis arrived at Carol's house he found her waiting for her father to come home from work, while Carol's mother was beautifying herself ready for the concert.

As soon as Carol's father arrived home, Dennis suddenly became very agitated and kept stammering and suggested, loudly: 'C . . . Carol, I . . . I . . . th . . . think we should j . . . join your p . . . parents and go to the c . . . c . . . concert tonight.'

'Oh!' said Carol, disappointedly. 'I didn't know you liked classical music, Dennis.'

'I don't,' hissed Dennis. 'But then, I didn't know your father was a chemist!'

770. Man: 'Have you been to bed with anyone?'
Girl (angrily): 'That's my business!'
Man: 'Oh! I didn't know you were a professional.'

771. 'My girlfriend says I'm handsome.'
'That's only because you feed her guide dog.'

772. 'And how is your son?' asked Mrs Goldberg.

'Oh, he is a constant joy to me,' replied Mrs Cohen.

'But how is that possible? Surely you know he is homo-sexual?'

'Yes, I know,' agreed Mrs Cohen, 'but recently he has been going out with such a nice Jewish lawyer.'

773. 'Is it true you've fallen in love with Dracula?'

'Yes. It was love at first bite.'

'My! How fangtastic!'

774. My first kiss was rather romantic. I was eleven at the time and had braces to help straighten my teeth. My girlfriend wore braces on her teeth, too – and it took the fire brigade half an hour to unhook us.

775. Claudia refuses to go out with married men – she insists they come in to her flat!

776. 'Oh, Brian, Mum wouldn't like it.'

'Your mother isn't going to get it!'

777. 'I've just become engaged,' said Sally, flashing her ring around the office.

'Yes,' said one of her colleagues, Kathy. 'The person who gave it to you is about six feet tall, has medium length brown hair, blue eyes, and a small tattoo in the shape of a butterfly on his right shoulder.'

'Fantastic, Sherlock Holmes!' exclaimed Sally. 'You can tell all that by just looking at the ring?'

'Certainly,' replied Kathy. 'It's the one I gave him back six months ago.'

778. Pretty young girl: 'What are we going to do today?'

Young man: 'How about a drive in the country?'

Pretty young girl: 'Will there be any kissing and cuddling and parking in lonely lanes and all that sort of thing?'

Young man: 'Certainly not!'

Pretty young girl: 'Then what are we going for?'

779. Young man to attractive young girl: 'I'd like to see you in a two-piece outfit – slippers!'

780. The nurse ended her romance with William because she felt she had been deceived.

William had told her that they had a lot in common as he frequently had to deal with poor hearts and livers. She thought he was a doctor – now she's found out he works in a butcher's shop.

781. 'Why do you want to marry Elizabeth?' asked Jonathan. 'Is she pregnant? Has she won a fortune on the lottery?'

'Neither,' replied Steven. 'I love her.'

'Oh,' said Jonathan, 'I thought there would be a catch in it.'

782. 'I saw you! I saw what you got up to last night!' said little Emily when her big sister's boyfriend came to visit.

'Oh!' said the boy, blushing. 'If you don't tell your parents I'll give you five pounds.'

'That's very generous,' replied Emily. 'All the others only offered me a pound.'

783. Greg had asked if he could marry Mr Brown's daughter.

'Would you still love her as much if she was poor?' asked Mr Brown, who was a self-made multi-millionaire.

'Of course, sir!' replied Greg, with feeling.

'Then I'm not happy about you marrying her,' replied Mr Brown. 'I don't want a fool in the family.'

784. Fred is extremely broadminded – he's got nothing else on his mind.

785. Young man: 'Oh, my gorgeous, sweetest darling! Am I the first man you've ever been to bed with?'

Young girl: 'Of course you are! Why do all you men always ask the same stupid question?'

S

SADIST
786. A sadist is someone who would put a drawing-pin on an electric chair.

SAILING
787. Suddenly, out at sea in our small sailing boat, we heard a loud noise: 'Croak, croak' it went. 'Croak, croak.' It was a frog-horn.

SALES PEOPLE
788. One door-to-door salesman does very well by using the opening line: 'Can I interest you in something your neighbour said you couldn't possibly afford?'

789. 'Humpkins!' boomed the boss. 'When I told you to fire the salesmen with enthusiasm, I did *not* want you to sack them all enthusiastically!'

790. The only orders the new trainee door-to-door salesman got were 'go away' and 'get out.'

SCHOOL
791. When I was a boy at school and studying biology the teacher suddenly picked on me and said: 'Boy! Why is mother's

milk better than other milk.'

I was so flustered that all I could think of to say was: 'Mother's milk comes in more attractive containers.'

792. 'Brian,' said the kindergarten teacher, 'I know you like nursery rhymes so I'm sure you can tell me why the cow jumped over the moon.'

Brian thought for a moment, then said: 'Was it because the milkmaid had icy cold hands?'

793. 'Susan!' said the teacher. 'Why did you just let out that awful yell?'

'Please miss,' said Susan, 'I've just hit my fumb wiv a 'ammer.'

'Susan,' responded the teacher, 'the word is "thumb", not "fumb".'

'Yes miss,' said Susan, 'but as well as 'itting my thumb I also 'it my thinger.'

794. Teacher: 'When I was your age I could name all the Presidents of America in the right order.'

Jason: 'Sir, was that because when you were my age there had only been two or three Presidents?'

795. 'Dad, I only got one question wrong in the maths exam at school today,' said the small boy.

'That's good,' replied the father. 'How many questions were there?'

'Thirty.'

'You did very well to get twenty-nine right.'

'Not really,' said the son, 'I couldn't answer twenty-nine of them at all.'

796. Teacher: 'What is the difference between the death rate in Victorian England and the present day?'

Pupil: 'It's the same, sir. One per person.'

797. Religious knowledge teacher: 'Now, Timothy, where do naughty boys and girls go?'

Timothy: 'Behind the bicycle shed in the playground.'

798. When I went knocking on doors asking for donations for a new school swimming pool, one peculiar person gave me a bucket of water.

799. Teacher: 'Now, Susan, can you tell me where God lives?'

Susan: 'Miss, I think he lives in the bathroom.'

Teacher: 'In the bathroom! Why do you think that?'

Susan: 'Because every morning I can hear my father knock on the bathroom door and say: "God, are you still in there?"'

800. The little girl was accused of cheating during the biology examination – the teacher found her counting her breasts.

801. School teacher: 'Can you stand on your head?'

Pupil: 'No. I can't get my feet up high enough.'

802. 'Hello,' said the school teacher, answering the phone. 'This is Miss Engels of Form Two of Mudleigh Junior School.'

'Hello,' said the voice on the phone. 'I'm phoning to tell you that Jim Brown is sick and won't be coming to school today.'

'Oh, I *am* sorry to hear that,' commented the teacher. 'Who is that speaking?'

The voice on the telephone replied: 'This is my father.'

803. Teacher: 'Now, Sarah, can you tell me what a skeleton is?'

Sarah: 'Yes, sir! A skeleton is a set of bones with the person scraped off.'

804. Teacher: 'If you stood facing due south, your back was north, what would be on your right hand?'

Schoolgirl: 'Fingers.'

805. Teacher: 'How many sheep does it take to make a man's jersey?'

Small boy: 'I don't know. I didn't know sheep could knit.'

806. Teacher: 'Patricia, can you tell me at which battle Nelson died?'

Patricia: 'His last one, miss.'

807. Religious knowledge teacher: 'Now, children, I've just described all the pleasures of Heaven. Hands up all those who want to go there?'

All the children put their hands up, except for Debbie.

Religious knowledge teacher: 'Debbie, why don't you want to go to Heaven?'

Debbie (tearfully): 'I'd like to go, miss, but me mum said I had to come straight home after school.'

808. Little Simon was the school swot – the other kids used to pick him up and bash flies with him.

809. What tickets did the babies sell at the school summer fête?

Rattle tickets.

810. The small boy in the school in China was surprised when his teacher suddenly loomed over him and demanded: 'Are you chewing gum?'

'No,' replied the small boy, 'I'm Chiu N Fung.'

811. Teacher: 'Wendy, can you put "defeat", "deduct", "defence", and "detail" in a sentence?'

Wendy: 'Yes, miss. De feet of de duck gets under de fence before de tail.'

812. Woman: 'Tell me, Des, how do you like school?'

Des: 'Closed.'

813. A friend of mine has a fifteen-year-old son at school in

London. She's very worried about his progress. Although his teacher gave him an 'A' in multi-cultural assimilation, an 'A' in psycho-social awareness and another 'A' in organizational behaviourism – my friend wonders when her son is going to learn how to read and write.

814. Teacher: 'Susan, give me a sentence beginning with "I".'
Susan: 'I is . . .'
Teacher (angrily): 'Susan! How many more times do I have to tell you! You must *always* say "I am"!'
Susan: 'All right, miss. I am the letter in the alphabet after H.'

815. The biology teacher in school asked: 'What is a blood count?'
John promptly replied: 'Is it Count Dracula?'

816. I used to have a teacher at school who kept going on and on insisting that five kilos of feathers weighed the same as five kilos of lead. So one day I emptied a five kilo bag of feathers over his head and then dropped a five kilo bag of lead on him. He was rather quiet after that.

817. Teacher: 'Now, James, if you bought twenty-five dough-nuts for one pound, what would each one be?'
James: 'Unless it was in a dream, stale or mouldy. They would have to be, at that ridiculous price.'

818. Teacher: 'Samantha, where did you learn to swim so well?'
Samantha: 'In the water.'

819. Teacher: 'Now, Robert, can you tell me the name of a bird that cannot fly?'
Robert: 'A roast chicken, sir.'

820. Teacher: 'Simon, did your parents help you with this homework?'
Simon: 'No, miss – I got it wrong all by myself this time.'

821. The two little girls were talking at school during playtime.

'Do you know how old teacher is?' asked Janice.

'No,' replied Sybil, 'but I know how to find out.'

'Oh, how?'

'Take off her knickers.'

'Take off her knickers!' exclaimed Janice. 'How will *that* tell us.'

'Well, in my knickers it says "4 to 6 years".'

SCIENTISTS

822. A scientist in Oxford has spent years trying to cross a pheasant with a guitar – he wants the pheasants to make music when they are plucked.

823. If rocket scientists are all so clever, why can they only count backwards, 10, 9, 8, 7 . . . ?

SCOTTISH

824. Did you hear about the Scotsman who died of a broken heart? He was tired of reading jokes about how mean the Scots are so he went into his nearest pub and ordered a round for everyone.

'That's very kind of you, sir,' commented the barman. 'There's almost fifty people in here. I didn't know you Jews were so generous.'

825. The Scotsman was visiting in London for the day and called upon a lady of pleasure in Soho and, after he had partaken of her bodily delights, he gave her two thousand pounds.

'Why, that's incredibly generous of you!' exclaimed the surprised lady. 'No man has ever before given me so much. And yet, from your accent you sound Scottish. Which part of Scotland do you come from?'

'From Edinburgh,' replied the Scotsman.

'How fantastic! My father works in Edinburgh.'

'I know,' said the Scotsman. 'When your father heard I was coming to London he asked me to bring you a share of his lottery winnings – two thousand pounds.'

826. The difference between a Scotsman and an Englishman can easily be discovered by letting loose a cow in their front gardens.

An Englishman will wail to his wife: 'Come quick and help me get rid of this horrible cow that's eating my prize lawn!'

The Scotsman will call to his wife: 'Come quick and bring a bucket – there's a cow on the lawn and it wants milking.'

827. The shy English girl on her first visit to Scotland nervously went up to a handsome young Scot who was wearing his national costume and asked: 'Excuse me speaking to a stranger, but I've always been curious. Please can you tell me what is worn under the kilt?'

The Scotsman smiled and said: 'Nothing is worn – everything is in excellent condition.'

828. The Englishman was in a restaurant in Scotland when he was suddenly attacked by a severe burst of coughing and sneezing – and he sneezed so violently that his false teeth flew out of his mouth and dropped to the floor, where they broke at the feet of a Scotsman.

'Don't worry, sir,' said the Scotsman. 'My brother will soon get you a new pair and at far less cost than an English dentist would charge. And he can provide a suitable set almost immediately.'

The Englishman couldn't believe his luck and gladly accepted the Scotsman's offer.

The Scotsman left the restaurant and returned nine minutes later with a pair of false teeth which he handed to the Englishman.'

'Fantastic!' exclaimed the Englishman, trying the teeth. 'They fit perfectly. Your brother must be a very clever dentist.'

'Oh, he's not a dentist,' replied the Scotsman. 'He's an undertaker.'

SECRETARIES

829. The sweet young secretary is busy applying make-up when the phone rings. She picks up the phone and a voice says: 'Is Mr Schwartz in yet?'

'No,' replies the secretary, 'he hasn't even been in yesterday yet.'

830. My secretary has only been working for me for two weeks and already she's a month behind.

831. His secretary thinks she's clever. She's joined as many unions as possible so she gets more chances of being called out on strike.

832. Senior civil servant: 'Did you phone my wife as I asked you to?'

Secretary: 'Certainly, sir. I told her you would be late home from the office due to an unexpected conference.'

Senior civil servant: 'And what did she say?'

Secretary: 'Can I rely on that?'

833. Secretary to an irate gentleman on the phone: 'Oh! Didn't you get our letter – I'm about to post it now.'

834. The angry employer was berating his sweet young secretary: 'Who told you that you could have the morning off just to go shopping? And now you have the cheek to ask for a salary increase – merely because you came with me as my assistant to the conference in Brussels last weekend! Who gives you encouragement for such fantastic ideas?'

Secretary: 'My legal adviser, sir.'

835. The boss leaned over his secretary, who was busily

painting her fingernails, and said: 'Miss Ruggles, I'd like to compliment you on your work – but when are you going to do any?'

836. Mavis: 'On the way to work this morning a man stopped me in the street and showed me the lining of his raincoat.'

Claudia: 'Are you sure he only wanted you to see his raincoat?'

Mavis: 'Oh, yes! He wasn't wearing anything else.'

837. When I arrived for work this morning, my secretary said: 'I can see you've had another quarrel with your wife.'

'Oh,' I said, rather stunned. 'How did you know that?'

'Because,' she replied, 'the kitchen knife is still stuck in your back.'

838. The young secretary, Dawn, used to tell such long, complicated and involved jokes to her colleagues in the office that they were often to be found asleep at the crack of Dawn.

839. I once said to my delightful young secretary: 'I just don't know what to do. What can I give to a valued client – a man who has expensive cars, an art collection worth millions, homes in London, Dorset, Switzerland, and the USA. He's a man with just about everything. What can I possibly give him?'

My secretary looked at me, smiled, and said: 'You're welcome to give him my phone number.'

840. My new secretary seems to think that all my correspondence is private and confidential: all the letters she types look as if she's taken them down in shorthand and typed them while wearing a blindfold.

841. Personnel Manager: 'How well can you type?'

Young secretary: 'My typing isn't very good – but I can erase at sixty-five words per minute!'

842. Fred: 'My secretary is a biblical secretary.'

John: 'A biblical secretary? What's that?'

Fred: 'One who believes in filing things according to the Bible saying: "seek and ye shall find".'

843. Personnel Manager: 'Can you do shorthand?'

Young secretary: 'Yes. But it takes me longer.'

844. His secretary is a miracle worker – it's a miracle if she works.

845. One boss had to fire eleven secretaries because of mistakes they wouldn't make.

846. I recently had to fire my secretary for pulling funny faces – the people didn't like it when she grabbed them and pulled their faces.

847. My new secretary seems to like wearing clothes that bring out the bust in her.

848. The young secretary changed her job due to men trouble. There weren't any men in her office.

849. Secretary: 'Please, Mr Jenkins, can I have two weeks off work?'

Mr Jenkins: 'What for?'

Secretary: 'I'm getting married.'

Mr Jenkins: 'But you've only just returned from your three week summer holiday! Why didn't you get married then?'

Secretary: 'What? And ruin my summer holiday?'

850. Mrs Jones: 'I'm Mr Jones's wife.'

Beautiful young secretary: 'Are you? I'm his secretary.'

Mrs Jones: '*Were* you?'

SELF EMPLOYED

851. Now I work for myself I find the greatest difficulty is when I phone to say I'm sick I don't know whether or not to believe myself.

SEX

852. A couple I know were having trouble with their love life so they went to seek professional help.

They were advised to put more variety into their sex lives – so now he tries to juggle and she does magic tricks while they make love.

853. A friend of mine was in New York and was approached by a prostitute.

'Would you like a good time?' asked the woman.

'How much?' asked my friend.

'What do you think I'm worth?' asked the prostitute.

'Fifty dollars?' suggested my friend.

'Cheapskate!' snapped the prostitute. 'You only get ugly trash for that sort of money!'

Later that evening my friend was with his wife waiting for a taxi outside the hotel. The prostitute happened to walk by and, as she did so, she hissed: 'See! I told you fifty dollars would only get you ugly trash!'

854. The slightly worried parents inquired of their son how the lesson on sex went that day. They were hoping that the teacher had not been too 'progressive'.

The boy gave a somewhat bored reply: 'Oh,' he said, 'it was useless – we only had the theory today!'

855. I was in a chemist's shop this morning and a very nervous young man came in and asked for a packet of anti-sickness pills and a packet of contraceptives.

The shop assistant looked at the trembling young man, smiled, and said: 'If it makes you sick, why do it?'

856. The only reason Keith's wife says he is good in bed is because she is very houseproud and when he makes love he doesn't disturb the sheets and blankets.

857. Albert was disappointed with his wife. Almost every night she had a headache, or was too tired, or made some other excuse not to make love.

In desperation, knowing how much his wife loved money, he told her: 'I'll put a ten pound note in the top drawer of your dressing table every time we make love.'

Soon, Albert was happy and his wife delighted in taking the ten pound notes from him for her passionate work.

Then one day Albert happened to open the top drawer of the dressing table and saw a bundle of ten pound notes and another bundle of £20 notes – plus a number of £50 notes.

'Where did all this money come from?' asked Albert. 'I only give you ten pound notes.'

'Well, dear,' said his wife, 'not everyone is as mean as you.'

858. Alison wanted to make sure that her first experience of sleeping with her boyfriend was a success, so she asked her best friend for advice.

'Why not go to a fish restaurant,' said the friend, 'and get your boyfriend to have some oysters? They are supposed to increase the sexual appetite. About half a dozen oysters should be enough.'

The next day the friend asked Alison: 'How did it go?'

'Well,' replied Alison, blushing, 'only three of the oysters seem to have worked.'

859. When Sally came home from the office unexpectedly early one day she found her handsome young husband in bed with a sixty-five-year-old woman. Sally was horrified.

Sally's husband looked up at her and said: 'Darling, this is the lady who provided your Porsche, and that nice diamond ring I gave you last week, and . . .'

'Oh,' said Sally. 'Sorry I interrupted. And can I have a necklace to match my ring?'

860. Mrs Green was outraged. She had caught the nubile young cook kissing and cuddling in the kitchen with Mr Green.

'If it happens again,' said Mrs Green, 'I'll have to get another cook.'

'Oh,' replied the cook, 'I wish you would. Your husband's always said he'd fancied it with two of us.'

861. Mr Smith was always so busy working that he never had much time to spend with his son.

Then, on his son's seventeenth birthday, Mr Smith managed to get away from his office to take his son for a birthday lunch at an expensive restaurant.

'Cor!' said the son when one of the waitresses took their coats. 'Look at the size of her boobs. I wonder what she's like in bed?'

Mr Smith was rather alarmed at his son's comments, but they were soon seated in the restaurant and father and son exchanged gossip and news.

Just as they were about to leave the restaurant, an attractive young woman entered.

'Wow!' exclaimed Mr Smith's son in a loud voice. 'Her boobs are fantastic. I really fancy her.'

Mr Smith was embarrassed. His son appeared to have turned into an uncouth, chauvinistic yob. Maybe the boy's school was to blame.

Thus it was that Mr Smith's son was removed from the local school and sent away to the upper form in one of Britain's most expensive public schools. It was surely not too late for the boy to learn some manners.

On his son's eighteenth birthday Mr Smith took his son to the same restaurant as before – and Mr Smith was delighted at the way his son behaved. He was polite, well-mannered, and did not make uncouth remarks about the waitresses but treated them with charm and was a perfect gentleman.

The son talked of his plans for university, and Mr Smith was just about to comment on the amazing transformation of his son into a man with excellent behaviour – surely the work of the public school – when the son looked at one of the waiters and said: 'Look at that! Isn't that a cute bottom? I wonder what he's like in bed.'

862. Although she was only the architect's daughter, she let the borough surveyor.

863. Clare was also known as 'Good Time' by her friends – because she was the good time that was had by all.

864. My marriage to Charles was a mistake. When he was just a boyfriend I thought he said he was over-sexed. Now I'm married to him, I realise I must have misheard him say he was over sex.

SEXTANT

865. The handsome young man was about to set off on a round-the-world yacht trip when his sextant was stolen.

He went into a shop on the quay and asked the new, attractive young female assistant: 'Do you have a sextant?'

'Why do it in a tent?' she asked. 'You can come back to my flat if you like.'

SHAKESPEARE

866. One day William Shakespeare was finding it difficult to concentrate on his writing work. Inspiration seemed to have deserted him.

Then, as he sat gnawing his pencil he glanced at it and suddenly creative thoughts rushed into his head and he began to write: '2B or not 2B . . .'

867. What would Shakespeare be doing if he was alive today?

Shouting and scratching at the lid on his coffin.

SHOOTING

868. I told my wife that we had been invited on a shooting weekend in Scotland.

'Oh good!' she said. 'Now I can see those strange birds that wear trousers.'

'Strange birds that wear trousers?' I asked.

'Yes,' she replied. 'People are always saying they shoot pheasants in braces.'

SHOPPING

869. Customer: 'Please do you have a dress that would match the colour of my eyes?'

Honest salesgirl: 'I'm sorry, madam, .but they don't make material in bloodshot.'

870. Tailor: 'Your suit will be ready in six weeks, sir.'

Customer: 'Six weeks! But God made the whole world in only six days!'

Tailor: 'Quite true, sir. But look what state the world is in.'

871. In a record shop there was a notice stating: 'Mendelssohn's Organ Works'. Underneath this notice someone had pinned a note on which was written: 'So does mine'.

872. A woman went into a hardware shop and asked the assistant if he had long nails.

'Certainly!' he replied. 'But don't ask me to scratch your back with them. I've heard that tired old joke too many times.'

'I wasn't going to tell a joke,' said the woman. 'Of course I want to buy real nails, not fingernails. Can I buy some?'

'Certainly, madam,' replied the assistant. 'How long do you want them?'

The woman sighed and replied: 'At least a few years. They're to repair the kids' rabbit hutch.'

873. A shopkeeper was held up by a man waving a bunch of flowers at him in a threatening manner. It was robbery with violets.

874. 'Do you sell dogs' meat?'
'Certainly – if they come here with their owner.'

875. People in Britain are becoming much stronger. Twenty years ago it would take two men to carry £20 of supermarket shopping. Now, even a small child can carry it.

876. I went to the perfume counter in a department store and asked to see and smell some different types of perfume. The assistant asked me: 'Is the perfume for your wife, sir – or would you like to see something more expensive?'

877. A man bought a bath and was just leaving the shop with his purchase when the shop assistant called: 'Do you want a plug?'
'Why?' asked the man. 'Is it electric?'

878. Business in some London shops is now so slow that when I picked up a bracelet in a jewellery shop and asked the young lady manager: 'Would you take anything off for cash?' she replied: 'For fifty pounds you can see me topless. For one hundred pounds I'll take everything off.'

879. Customer: 'I want a pen that writes underwater.'
Shop assistant: 'Wouldn't you like it to write other words, too?'

880. My wife is so stupid she went window shopping the other day – and came home with five windows.

881. The massive new development in the town centre included a multi-storey car park, a luxury hotel and a major shopping complex which included several department stores.

The largest department store was extremely crowded and, as the lift attendant closed the doors, he called: 'Which floors, please?'

A young man standing near the back of the lift cried out: 'Ballroom!'

'Oh, I'm sorry,' said a large lady in front of him. 'I didn't know I was crushing you that much.'

882. Yesterday I went shopping with my girlfriend and she went into the chemist's shop and asked if they had any mirrors.

'Do you want a hand mirror?' asked the sales assistant.

'No,' replied my girlfriend, 'I don't want to look at my hands in it, I want one I can see my face in.'

883. He bought a piece of antique furniture quite cheaply from a seafood restaurant. It was Fish and Chippendale.

884. Retired Army colonel: 'I'd like some pepper, my good man.'

Shop assistant: 'Certainly, sir! What sort would you like – white or black pepper?'

Retired Army colonel: 'Neither. I want toilet pepper!'

885. I wouldn't say my sister is stupid, but the other day she went into a pet shop and bought some bird seed. She thinks that if she plants it she'll grow a bird.

886. Customer: 'Can I have a crocodile handbag, please?'

Shop assistant; 'I'm sorry, madam, but we don't sell handbags for crocodiles. What would they put in them – paper tissues for tears?'

887. After searching all over the department store's furnishing section, a woman sighed: 'They don't make antiques like they used to!'

888. 'Is this a second-hand shop?'
'Yes.'
'Please can you fit one on my alarm clock?'

SISTERS

889. My sister was asked if she'd like to be a baby sitter – but she said she thought it cruel to sit on babies.

890. My sister has visited another planet. This morning she trod on a chocolate bar and said she'd just set foot on Mars.

891. My sister isn't really fat – but when her boyfriend filled her shoe with champagne it took five bottles to do it.

892. I wouldn't say my sister was an ugly baby – but it was almost a year before my mother realized she had been putting the nappy on the wrong end.

SLEEP

893. When I asked a friend of mine if he ever woke up grumpy in the morning he said that he didn't have to – his wife had her own alarm clock.

894. When my brother was a small boy he once slept with his head under the pillow. When he woke up he found twenty-eight one-pound coins – and all his teeth were missing: the fairies had taken them.

895. Whenever I go to stay with people they always ask me how I slept. How do you think I slept? Do they think I'm odd or something? I sleep like everyone else – with my eyes closed.

896. The insomniac sheep could only get to sleep by counting people.

897. I'm very sleepy. I had to get up at the crack of yawn.

898. Last night I slept like a baby – I kept waking up and crying.

899. Last night I dreamt I was eating my pillow, so when I woke up I felt a bit down in the mouth.

SMOKING
900. I'm quite pleased with myself. I now only smoke three packets of cigarettes a day. I gave up cigarettes completely – I just smoke the packets.

901. My cousin is a chain smoker. She gave up cigarettes – now she only attempts to smoke chains.

SONGS FOR FISH AND ANIMALS
902. 'Mackerel The Knife.'

903. 'My Bear Lady.'

904. 'I've Got Ewe Under My Skin.'

905. 'Snake, Rattle And Mole.'

906. 'Weasel Overcome.'

907. 'Tie A Yellow Gibbon Round An Old Oak Tree.'

908. 'Whale Meet Again.'

909. 'Jack The Kipper.'

910. 'I'm Gonna Wash That Man Right Out Of My Bear.'

911. 'Hit The Road Yak.'

912. 'If You Were The Only Gill In The World.'

913. 'Red Snails In The Sunset.'

914. 'Amazing Plaice.'

915. 'Salmon Chanted Evening.'

916. 'Fly Me To Baboon.'

917. 'Mullet of Kintyre.'

918. 'Long And Winding Toad.'

SPEECH

919. A guarantee of freedom of speech is not much use unless there is another guarantee of freedom *after* the speech.

SPIES

920. The aspiring spy was being interviewed in Whitehall by a Secret Service Chief, who was explaining the sort of men he looked for.

'We need people who are more than just involved,' he said. 'In this game you have to be committed. It is rather like the difference between bacon and eggs. So far as the chicken is concerned with the production of this marvellous start to the day – well she *is* involved; but the pig, *he* is committed!'

921. 1st spy: 'I think Claude has become a mole.'
2nd spy: 'How do you know?'

1st spy: 'Because he's started eating worms and burying himself in the garden.'

STATISTICIAN
922. A statistician is a person who, if you've got your feet in the oven and your head in the refrigerator, will tell you that, on average, you're very comfortable.

SUNBURN
923. You only get really terrible sunburn if you bask for it.

SUPERSTITIOUS
924. I'm definitely *not* superstitious. It's bad luck to be superstitious.

T

TAXI DRIVERS

925. An Englishwoman and her young son were travelling in a taxi in New York, USA.

As the taxi passed a particularly seedy part of the city, the small boy was fascinated by the garishly made-up ladies who were walking along the streets accosting some of the male passers-by.

'What are those ladies doing?' asked the boy.

His mother blushed and said, somewhat embarrassed: 'I expect they are lost and are asking people for directions.'

The taxi driver overheard this, and said in a loud voice: 'Why don'tcha tell the boy the truth – in udda woids they're prostitutes.'

The woman blushed even deeper red, and her son asked: 'What are p . . . p . . . pros . . . what the driver said? Are they like other women? Do they have children?'

'Of course,' replied his mother. 'That's where New York taxi drivers come from.'

TELEPHONE

926. 'Why don't you answer the phone?'

'Because it's not ringing.'

'Why must you leave everything until the last minute?'

927. Over the phone some voices are very difficult to extinguish.

TELEPHONE BOXES

928. There I was, stranded in a strange town, and I urgently needed to use the public telephone.

Unfortunately, a rather plump lady was busily flipping through the pages of the phone book and so I could not get to the phone.

I waited patiently. Still the plump lady scanned the pages of the phone book.

After ten minutes, I grew a little exasperated (it's a small flower related to the tulip) and gently tapped the plump lady on the shoulder.

'Excuse me,' I said. 'Can I help you find a number in the phone book?'

'Oh,' she replied. 'I'm not exactly looking for a number. My daughter is expecting her first child next month and she's asked me to suggest some names for it. That's why I'm looking in the phone book – to see if I can find some nice-sounding names to suggest.'

TELEVISION

929. I refused to watch the new TV series about the life and times of Ethelred the Unready. It should not have been screened – there's much too much Saxon violence.

930. People say that with all the developments in television – cable, satellite, high definition TV – that TV will eventually completely replace newspapers. But have you ever tried to swat a fly with a television set?

TIME

931. It's easy to make time fly: just throw an alarm clock over your shoulder.

THEATRE

932. The last time I was in London I went to a theatre ticket office and the man in front of me in the queue asked the box office clerk: 'Can I have a ticket for tonight's performance?'

'Certainly sir,' replied the clerk. 'Would you like to be in the stalls?'

'No,' said the man. 'I'm not an animal – I want a proper seat.'

933. I've just got a speaking part in the theatre. I have to walk up and down saying: 'Programmes. Would anyone like a programme?'

934. I've just been to see a hit play – most of the cast were hit by rotten eggs and tomatoes.

TIDINESS
935. Mr Smith was fed up with his wife's insistence on absolute tidiness. He was not allowed to smoke cigarettes or cigars or a pipe at home. He had to take off his shoes before he entered the house.

His wife even made him comb his hair in the garden in case a spot of dandruff fell on the floor.

When he died, Mr Smith managed to get some revenge. His will stipulated that his ashes were to be scattered on the lounge carpet.

TRADE UNION
936. One trade union is now demanding that unskilled men get paid more than skilled men because the work is harder if people are not skilled to do it.

937. Then there was the trade union leader who used to tell bedtime stories to his children: 'Once upon a double time . . .'

TRAIN TRAVEL
938. 'Why did you become a driver for the railway?'

'It was the only way I was sure of getting a seat on a train.'

939. The only reason the railways in Britain print timetables is so passengers know how late their trains have been.

940. I wouldn't say my sister is desperate for a boyfriend, but when she went to the station and asked for a ticket from Bournemouth to London, the young male ticket clerk asked: 'Single?' – and she replied: 'Yes. Are you asking me for a date?'

U

941. A man on holiday in the USA was amazed at the way his host, a huge Texan, had everything so much larger than back home in England.

The car was as long as three English cars put together; the bedrooms were big enough to play a tennis match in; and the kitchen was so big it could cook enough to feed an Army.

The Englishman was very impressed with all this Texan greatness, but after he had been staying in his host's gigantic house for about a week he began to drink even more than he normally did back in England.

One night, after getting particularly drunk, the Englishman fell into his host's swimming pool. When the servants rushed to rescue him they found him screaming: 'Don't flush it! Don't flush it!'

942. We're continually hearing about the terrible crime rate in America, but is it true?

For example, when I arrived in New York a few months ago, a man sidled up to me and said: 'Want to buy a watch?'

'How much? I asked.

'Sssh!' said the man, 'the guy next to you is still wearing it.'

UNIVERSITY
943. The university had arranged for some 'practical sessions' for students who were studying for degrees in education with a

168

view to becoming teachers. The students had already received detailed instruction on how to cope with almost every situation.

One of the students was sent to a primary school where she was to spend several days teaching the youngsters.

On her second day at the school, the university student wanted to find out who was responsible for a suspicious pool of water near the blackboard. She remembered what one of her lecturers had instructed for dealing with such a situation, so she told all the children to shut their eyes so that whoever knew who was responsible for the puddle could step forward anonymously and write the offender's name on the blackboard.

Everyone, including the teacher, closed their eyes. Soon, a tip-toeing could be heard approaching the blackboard. After a few nasty squeaks with the chalk, the tip-toe could be heard going back to their seat.

When everyone opened their eyes, *another* pool of water had appeared – and on the blackboard was written: 'The phantom widdler strikes again!'

944. The university lecturer was speaking to an audience of townspeople. He was attempting to prove there was a definite connection between happiness and the amount of sex in people's lives.

To help prove his point, he asked those in the audience who indulged every night to raise their hands. Only five per cent did so, all laughing merrily.

He then asked how many indulged about once per week, and seventy per cent raised their hands, smiling contentedly as they did so.

Then the people who indulged once every month were asked to raise their hands, but it was noticeable that these people neither laughed nor smiled.

The lecturer felt that this proved his point – but to show how obvious this matter was, he asked those who only indulged once every year to raise their hands. A tall man at the back of the hall leapt from his chair, waving his hand and laughing loudly.

The lecturer was astonished at this apparent contradiction to his lecture, and he asked the man if he could explain why he was so happy.

The man replied: 'Certainly. It's tonight! It's tonight!'

USSR
945. In the old days of the USSR, all the history books used to have loose leaves.

V

VET

946. When the budgie got sick, my children insisted I took it to the vet for tweetment.

VITAMINS

947. The difference between a vitamin and a hormone is that you cannot hear a vitamin.

948. When I was a small boy my mother used to give me vitamins B1, B2, B6, B12 and B quiet.

W

WALK

949. Once I was out on a country walk in an area I'd never been to before. I enjoyed the beautiful scenery and soon I came to a stream – the other side of which was a country bakery from which came the delicious smell of fresh bread.

The stream was a bit too wide for me to jump across safely, but the water did not look too deep, although it was a bit muddy and I could not see the bottom.

A young girl was sitting by the side of the stream.

'Hello!' I said. 'Do you live near here?'

'Yes,' replied the girl.

'That's good,' I said. 'Then you can tell me how deep the stream is. Would I be able to walk across?'

'I think so,' replied the girl. 'The water isn't very deep.'

'Thanks,' I said, and stepped into the stream, only to sink into the water up to my neck.

'Hey!' I shouted to the girl, who was now giggling. 'I thought you said the water wasn't very deep.'

'I didn't know,' giggled the girl. 'I thought it was shallow. The water only manages to cover the legs of ducks and swans.'

WASP

950. My young son came rushing into my study shouting: 'I've been stung! I've been stung by a wasp!'

'Don't worry,' I soothed. 'I'll put some special cream on it.'

'That's no good,' said my son, 'the wasp has flown away and you'll never find it.'

WATCH

951. 'I've got an amazing watch. It only cost me five pounds.'
'Why is it so amazing?'
'Because every time I look at it I'm amazed it's still working.'

952. What goes 'tick, tock, woof'? A watch dog.

WEATHER

953. The hard pressed managing director had just returned from a gruelling overseas trip and was relaxing at home when the telephone rang. When he hung up almost at once his wife inquired who it was.

'Someone with the wrong number my love,' he said. 'He wanted to know if the coast was clear. So I suggested he telephone the Met. Office!'

WEDDING

954. The woman wearing an enormous flowery hat was stopped at the entrance to the church by one of the ushers.

'Are you a friend of the bride?' asked the usher.

'Of course not!' snapped the woman. 'I'm the groom's mother.'

955. I was a bit concerned on our wedding day when my husband stumbled over the words of his wedding vows, dropped the ring, and then whispered to the best man: 'Sorry! I'll do better next time.'

956. What is the point of being best man if you never get a chance to prove it?

957. A young lady I know in Hollywood has just arranged her wedding for seven o'clock in the morning – that way, if the marriage doesn't work out, she will still have most of the morning left.

WEDDING PRESENTS

958. My brother is so mean. Before I got married he promised us a food mixer as a wedding present, and I was so surprised at his unexpected generosity. On the wedding day, however, he handed me his carefully wrapped food mixer – a wooden spoon!

959. It was the woman's second marriage and her first husband was kind enough to send the happy couple a wedding gift of a carving set – two chisels and a hammer.

WEDDING RECEPTION

960. The bride had got a little drunk and was having some difficulty in making her speech of thanks for all the wonderful wedding gifts.

At the end of her speech she pointed rather unsteadily towards an electric coffee percolator, and said: 'And, finally, I'd like to thank my husband's parents for giving me such a lovely perky copulator.'

961. 'Psst!' said the slimy looking man to the groom. 'Do you have any photos of your wife in the nude?'

'Of course not!' growled the groom.

'Want to buy some?' asked the slimy looking man.

962. The happy couple proudly displayed all their wedding gifts at the reception – including an envelope from the groom's father marked 'Cheque for five thousand pounds'.

'Who is that strange man pointing at your father's cheque and laughing?' asked the bride.

The groom looked at the offending person, blushed, and said: 'My father's bank manager.'

WEIGHING MACHINE

963. Jack's wife stepped on the weighing machine which also produced a fortune reading on the other side of the weight indicator card.

Out popped the card, and Jack's wife said: 'It says I'm attractive, have a pleasing personality and can charm anyone I meet.'

'Huh!' muttered Jack, taking the card from his wife. 'Even the weight is wrong!'

WINTER

964. Winter is the time when it is too cold to do all the boring things that it was too hot or too wet to do in Summer.

965. I always know when Winter has arrived because that is when my neighbour returns my lawnmower.

WIVES

966. I used to miss my wife every time she went away for a week to visit her mother. But now I just get in a neighbour to nag me instead.

967. My wife isn't exactly fat and ugly, but whenever she goes to the doctor he tells her to open her mouth and say 'Moo!'

968. Fred: 'My wife converted me to religion.'

Bill: 'Your wife converted you to religion? How did she do that?'

Fred: 'Because I didn't believe in Hell until I married her!'

969. Jim is terribly sad. His wife has run off with his best friend – and he misses his friend terribly.

970. 'What's the trouble? You look really miserable.'

'It's Fiona, your wife.'

'My wife?'

'Yes. I'm afraid she's been unfaithful to both of us.'

971. I call my wife a wonder woman – I sometimes wonder if she's a woman.

972. I've got the most sexy, witty, creative, intelligent wife in the world . . . I just hope her husband doesn't know about it.

973. If my wife has nothing to wear, why does she need three giant wardrobes to keep it in?

974. My wife makes a good living curing people. She's so ugly she hires herself out to frighten people and cure them of hiccups.

975. Claude's wife is like the Mona Lisa – she's as flat as a canvas and should be in a museum.

976. My husband says he's going to dance on my grave when I die – so today I made a new will leaving instructions that I'm to be buried at sea.

977. My wife is a wonderful magician – she can turn anything into an argument.

978. Farmer's wife: 'I'm thinking of divorcing Joe.'

Mabel: 'But why?'

Farmer's wife: 'Because he smokes in bed.'

Mabel: 'Surely that's not sufficient reason? Only smoking in bed?'

Farmer's wife: 'Ah! But Joe smokes bacon.'

979. After spending a fortune on my wife for beauty treatments I can honestly say that the only thing that makes her look good is distance.

980. My wife is so jealous that when she couldn't find any female hairs on my coat she accused me of going out with bald-headed women.

981. Tom: 'There's one word that describes my wife: temperamental.'
John: 'In what way?'
Tom: 'She's fifty per cent temper and fifty per cent mental!'

982. I wouldn't say my wife has a big mouth, but she called me from London yesterday. I was in Southampton at the time and we don't *have* a telephone!

983. It's not that my wife was fat when I married her – it's just that when I carried her over the threshold I had to make two trips.

984. My wife has a stomach problem – she's grown so fat she can't fasten her blouse over her stomach.

985. Last night at the dinner dance my wife gave me a terrible kick that has left a nasty bruise. All I did was whisper to her that I thought her white tights looked a bit wrinkled. Unfortunately, she wasn't wearing any tights.

986. The easiest way to stop a runaway horse is to get my wife to place a bet on it.

987. The much-married actor told his new girlfriend that she shouldn't believe all the tales about his bad habits – they were just old wives' tales.

988. I've had to wear pink frilly knickers ever since my wife discovered a pair in my raincoat pocket.

989. 'Why do you call your wife Camera? Surely that's not her proper name?'

'Her real name is Gladys – but I call her Camera because she's always snapping at me.'

990. I think I've rather dropped myself in it. Early this morning, when I was not properly awake, my wife said: 'Darling, what would you do if I died?'

I stretched, yawned, and said: 'I don't know, dear. I love you much too much to want to think about awful things like that – especially so early in the morning.'

'But what would you do? Would you remarry?' asked my wife.

'I don't think so, dear,' I replied. 'You know I only have eyes for you. Who could possibly be as wonderful as you?'

I yawned again and then tried to go back to sleep for another few minutes, but my wife continued her questions. 'If you did remarry,' she said, 'would your new wife wear my rings and necklaces?'

'I don't think so,' I said, without thinking, 'Aurelia's got smaller fingers and a more delicate neck than you, dear.'

991. My wife has a better sense of judgment than I have – she chose me as her husband.

992. My wife insists she's not fat – just that she's three feet too short for her body.

993. My wife is so ugly, when we went on holiday to Africa even the mosquitoes wouldn't bite her.

994. My wife is thinking about going back to university. She's just heard that they've got a new course which she thinks is all about shopping – it's called buy-ology.

995. My wife is so fat, if she was a stripper she'd have to wear a G-rope.

996. Cuthbert's wife made him a millionaire. Before he

married her he was a multi-millionaire.

997. 'I hear your first two wives died of mushroom poisoning. And now you tell me your third wife has just died as a result of falling off a cliff. A bit strange, isn't it?'
'Not really. She refused to eat the poisoned mushrooms.'

998. My wife is so ugly that last night I got a phone call from a Peeping Tom pleading with me to get her to draw the curtains shut before she undresses for bed.

999. 'I didn't make love to my wife before we were married. Didn't believe in that sort of thing. Did you?'
'Don't know. What did you say your wife's name was?'

1000. My wife is so stupid she once took a tape measure to bed with her to try and discover how long she slept.

1001. John: 'My wife's a kleptomaniac.'
Richard: 'Is she taking anything for it?'

1002. My wife had plastic surgery last week – I cut off her credit card.

1003. 'Where did you get such a nice suit?'
'It was a present from my wife. I came home unexpectedly early from the office the other evening, and there it was – hanging over the back of a chair in the bedroom.'

1004. I wouldn't say my wife is a gossip – she just has a good sense of rumour.

1005. My wife and I have somewhat different political views, but I agreed to support her when she decided to appear before the selection committee of her local Party to see if she was a suitable candidate to be the next Member of Parliament for the area in which we live.

As part of the selection process, each candidate had to give a short campaigning speech.

My wife began: 'What this country needs is much more reform. We need Electoral Reform! Social Services Reform! Education Reform! European Community Reform!'

At this point I could not hold back the words any longer and had to shout: 'And chloroform!'

1006. My wife has a very clean mind – probably because she changes it every few minutes.

1007. My wife has a photographic mind – but it's a great pity it never developed.

1008. My wife is so conceited she only looks at me because she can see her own reflection in my spectacles.

1009. 'Darling, you have the face of a saint.'
  'Dearest, you say the sweetest things! Which saint?'
  'A Saint Bernard!'

1010. When Fred's wife was born they fired twenty-one guns. Unfortunately, they all missed.

1011. My wife is so ugly whenever she goes to the zoo she has to buy two tickets – one to get in, and one to get out.

1012. Clive: 'I can find my wife anywhere I go.'
  Robert: 'How?'
  Clive: 'All I have to do is open my wallet – and there she is.'

1013. A month ago my wife put mud all over her face to improve her looks. It improved them so much she hasn't taken the mud off yet.

1014. Wife: 'Do you have a good memory for faces?'
  Husband: 'Yes. Why?'

Wife: 'I've just broken your shaving mirror.'

1015. Adrian was, as usual, complaining about his wife. 'She's always breaking her promsies,' he said. 'Before we married she claimed she'd die for me – but she hasn't.'

1016. My wife has a memory like an elephant – and a face to match.

1017. My wife is such a snob she won't eat hot dogs unless they've been registered with the Kennel Club.

1018. My wife was so bad when she was a small girl that her parents ran away from home.

1019. My wife is in the mining business – she's always saying: 'That's mine! That's mine! And that's mine!'

1020. My young wife was arrested in one of those conservative foreign countries for wearing a bikini top that was far too small, even though the policeman who arrested her agreed with me that she had two fantastic excuses.

1021. My wife takes three hours to eat a plate of alphabet soup – she insists on eating it alphabetically.

1022. 'My wife is an Eighth Day Adventist.'
   'Don't you mean a Seventh Day Adventist?'
   'No – she's always late for everything.'

1023. My wife is so thin that it takes three of her to make a shadow. Once when she swallowed a prune she was rushed to the maternity hospital.

1024. It was breakfast one month after their marriage.
   'Darling,' said the wife. 'Will you love me when I'm old and wrinkled.'

The husband lowered his morning newspaper and said: 'Of course I do.'

1025. 'Susan has been married and divorced so many times to wealthy men she must be getting richer by decrees.'

1026. Whenever I argue with my wife we soon patch things up – like my black eye, my broken nose, broken arm . . .

1027. My wife doesn't really have a big mouth – but she once gave the kiss of life to a whale.

1028. As a wedding anniversary gift, Frank Smith bought his wife one of those answering machines that record telephone messages when you are out. The first day she got it she fitted it up to say: 'This is the Smith residence. Unfortunately, Mrs Smith is out but this machine will record your message. Please start your rumour or gossip now . . .'

WRITER
1029. Writer: 'I took up writing full-time about a year ago.'
    Friend: 'Have you sold anything?'
    Writer: 'Yes – my colour TV, all the furniture, the carpets, the house . . .'

X

X-RAY

1030. Brian had great problems finding a woman. Indeed, he found it difficult to get *anyone* to like him as his face was covered in acne and he had an incredibly irritating horse-like laugh which he appended to the end of almost every sentence.

Then, one day, he slipped on an icy pavement and was taken to hospital to be X-rayed for a suspected broken leg and wrist.

It was then that it happened. As the X-rays were being taken his eyes met those of the radiographer and they fell in love – she knew what was in him.

Z

ZEBRAS

1031. Farmer Giles went to the sales to buy himself a horse. Unfortunately that day there were no horses but the final lot to come up was a zebra and even though he knew that no one had ever trained a zebra to do anything before, he decided to make a low offer. Naturally he got it. Knowing what he knew he immediately told the zebra that when he got back to the farm he was to go around all the animals and chat to them about their work and then decide what he could do best. He warned the zebra that if he did not become a useful animal within six weeks he would be packed off to the abattoir.

So the zebra lost no time in talking to the animals. He asked the hen first, what did she do? 'Oh well,' cackled the hen, 'I peck around in the farmyard here, pick up a few worms and as long as I lay an egg every day old Giles leaves me alone – it's a good life really.' 'I don't think I would like that,' said the zebra, 'I think I will go and talk to the pig and see what he does.'

He explained to the pig the stern command that he had had from Giles and asked him what he did. 'Oh, I enjoy myself,' the pig snorted, 'I snuffle around in this mud and he gives me lots of hot potato peelings and good food and doesn't ask me for much. The only thing that worries me is that a few of my brothers have disappeared recently and I don't think what happens to them is terribly good news. Still, I live in the hope that my turn is yet a long way off.'

The zebra thought this was a little uncertain for him so he continued with his inquiries by asking the bull what he did for a living. The bull snorted impatiently, 'If you take those silly pyjamas off,' he roared, 'I will show you!'

ZOO

1032. The two apes in the zoo were a very rare species of Pongidae and the zoo was keen that they should breed.

The apes were given a special cage equipped with every comfort: swings, ropes, trees, pond. But still they refused to mate.

Their diet was changed and they had the best fruit and other food that money could buy. The two apes, while friendly towards each other, declined to mate.

After eighteen months of carefully observing the apes for signs of sexual activity, the zoologists were still disappointed. The apes were given fertility pills to increase their sexual appetite – but the apes remained just friends.

'Perhaps they don't know what to do,' suggested their keeper. 'They are pretty intelligent creatures, so why don't we put a TV in their cage and show them videos of apes making love?'

'Good idea,' said the zoo director, and the TV was soon installed.

Each afternoon, just after the last visitor had left the zoo, the apes were shown the sexually explicit videos while their keeper secretly watched.

Although the videos failed to stimulate the apes into action, their keeper's wife was amazed at the way her husband carried her off to the bedroom immediately he arrived home each day.

1033. The zoo had fallen on hard times. The numbers of visitors to the zoo had fallen dramatically over the years and now the zoo was facing bankruptcy. It would have to close.

The zoo owners decided to sell all the animals and birds in the zoo at auction in an attempt to raise as much money as possible towards the zoo's debts.

Bidding was particularly good for one of the parrots. The

auctioneer started the bidding at £100 and the price rapidly rose to £1,000 and the parrot was eventually sold to a young man for £1,250.

As the successful bidder wrote out a cheque, he said to the auctioneer's assistant: 'I think I got carried away with the excitement of it all. I didn't intend to pay all that much for the parrot, but as the price went up and up it seemed the bird must be really good. I hope that for £1,250 the parrot can talk a lot.'

'He certainly can,' said the auctioneer's assistant. 'Who do you think was bidding against you?'

1034. Amelia was recently forcibly ejected from the zoo because she fed the rabbits. She fed them to the lions.

1035. 'Daddy,' said the young camel. 'Why do I have soft, wide, two-toed feet?'

'It makes it easier for you to walk on a sandy desert,' replied the father. 'Feet like ours don't sink deep into the sand.'

'Why do I have such long eyelashes?' asked the young camel.

'To keep the sand out of your eyes,' responded the father.

'Why do I have nostrils that I can close?'

'For the same reason,' explained the father. 'Being able to close your nostrils is very useful if there is a sandstorm. And, before you ask, the reason why you have a hump on your back is so that you can store fat for use when travelling long distances across deserts without food or water.'

'But daddy,' said the young camel, 'if I have all these things to help me survive in the desert – why am I in a city zoo?'

1036. Mr and Mrs Smith and their young daughter were on a visit to the zoo. Mr Smith was a fitness fanatic: he went jogging for five miles every day, lifted weights, did all sorts of exercises. He was also incredibly conceited.

When they reached the cage containing the monkeys, the Smiths' daughter was entranced by the way the creatures jumped from branch to branch and did all sorts of acrobatics.

'You should see me in the gym,' said Mr Smith. 'The stuff I

do makes those monkeys look pretty boring. I do all sorts of leaps, somersaults and jumping from bar to bar and climbing ropes.'

At the cage containing the leopards, Mr Smith boasted of his running successes and the medals he had won in various athletics events. He could, he said, even run faster than the average leopard.

By the time they reached the owls, Mrs Smith had grown rather weary of her husband's comments. Surely Mr Smith wouldn't feel the need to demonstrate any superiority over a humble owl. But he did.

'You know,' said Mr Smith, 'an owl has got pretty good eyesight at night – but compared to me it's not as good. Drinking lots of carrot juice, and with lots of practice and training my eyes, I've developed excellent night vision: better than that poor owl.'

When the Smith family reached the zebra enclosure, Mrs Smith was a bit surprised to find that two of the zebras were about to make love.

'Daddy,' said the Smiths' young daughter, 'what is that long thing between the back legs of one of the zebras?'

For once, Mr Smith was embarrassed and he blushed as he said: 'Oh, that's nothing.'

'Huh!' said Mrs Smith. 'There you go – boasting again!'

1037. The male gymnast needed to raise money to support himself while in training and to pay for his travel and hotel expenses during overseas competitions.

He was therefore delighted when he was asked to participate in a secret mission for a month during the peak tourist season at the local zoo.

The zoo's much loved ape had just died. It was a great tourist attraction as he was extremely acrobatic: jumping from branch to branch, swinging from ropes, doing somersaults. The zoo did not want to admit that the ape had died as many people came to the zoo just to watch the ape. Without such an attraction, the number of visitors would decline – and the zoo needed every paying customer it could get in order to survive.

The gymnast was therefore asked to dress up in the ape's skin and act like the ape: tumbling, swinging and being extremely energetic.

The gymnast loved this new work and all went well until the last week of his engagement. After a particularly energetic swing on the rope he accidentally let go and hurtled out of the cage and into the lion's enclosure.

As he landed, he looked up to see a fierce lion approaching. He started to scream for help, but the lion put a mighty paw across the gymnast's mouth and hissed: 'Sssh! Do you want us *both* to lose our summer jobs?'

1038. The little boy on his first visit to the zoo followed all the signs. He saw the sign which said 'To the Elephants' and enjoyed watching them, then followed the sign 'To the Penguins' and found their antics amusing; but when he followed the sign 'To the Exit' he was disappointed at finding himself back in the street outside the zoo without seeing the Exit animal.

1039. Some of the animals in the zoo disliked being looked at by hordes of noisy visitors every day. They knew there was nothing they could do about their situation, but to pass away the time in their rather cramped cages and enclosures they would sometimes wonder what it would be like if they could take some revenge on their human tormentors.

'I'd like to eat that fat actor who is always bringing his stupid children to drop coins on my head in a feeble attempt to see if I'm awake or asleep,' said one of the crocodiles.

'I agree,' replied another crocodile, 'although as I'm Jewish I wouldn't be able to eat such ham. But there are other equally dreadful people whom I could cheerfully chomp.'

'So could I,' agreed a lion. 'But the tastiest meat would probably be that well-known politician. I'd love to give him one big bite to let all the wind out of him – then what was left would be delicious: soft, fleshy and absolutely no backbone.'

WEDDING SPEECHES

This book consists entirely of wedding speeches. There are 15 speeches for the bridegroom, 15 for the best man, 12 for the bride's father (along with another 8 suitable for occasions when the bride's father does not speak), and 15 which are suitable for other relations and friends who may want to say something.

WEDDING ETIQUETTE PROPERLY EXPLAINED

Tells you everything you need to plan the wedding day with complete confidence. From the ceremony, the reception, the flowers and the cake, to the invitations, the gifts and the legalities of marriage – the book explains wedding etiquette clearly, and will give you the ideas to make any wedding day a complete success.

BEST MAN'S DUTIES

If you've been asked to be the best man at a wedding and aren't sure what the task entails, you need this book. It's a comprehensive guide describing in detail *all* the duties expected of a best man. It will answer all your queries and help you to ensure that the wedding is a great success.

YOUR VOICE
How To Enrich It, And Develop It For Speaking, Acting And Everyday Conversation

This is a simple but valuable guide for those who want to polish and improve their most potent means of communication: the voice. It will help all its readers to achieve peak performance with clear, dynamic and persuasive speech.

THE RIGHT WAY TO CONDUCT MEETINGS

This book is for the Chairmen of voluntary organisations, and for all those who want to understand procedure in councils, debates and conferences. It explains the pivotal role of the Chairman in getting the business completed quickly, efficiently, and without loss of humour.

THE ASTUTE PRIVATE INVESTOR

Kevin Goldstein-Jackson shows what to look for in a share, how to assess company reports and new issues and how to make money in a slump. He'll help you decide which shares to buy – and when to sell – and how to beat the professionals at their own game.

RIGHT WAY
PUBLISHING POLICY

HOW WE SELECT TITLES

RIGHT WAY consider carefully every deserving manuscript. Where an author is an authority on his subject but an inexperienced writer, we provide first-class editorial help. The standards we set make sure that every **RIGHT WAY** book is practical, easy to understand, concise, informative and delightful to read. Our specialist artists are skilled at creating simple illustrations which augment the text wherever necessary.

CONSISTENT QUALITY

At every reprint our books are updated where appropriate, giving our authors the opportunity to include new information.

FAST DELIVERY

We sell **RIGHT WAY** books to the best bookshops throughout the world. It may be that your bookseller has run out of stock of a particular title. If so, he can order more from us at any time – we have a fine reputation for "same day" despatch, and we supply any order, however small (even a single copy), to any bookseller who has an account with us. We prefer you to buy from your bookseller, as this reminds him of the strong underlying public demand for **RIGHT WAY** books. Readers who live in remote places, or who are house-bound, or whose local bookseller is unco-operative, can order direct from us by post.

FREE

If you would like an up-to-date list of all **RIGHT WAY** titles currently available, send a stamped self-addressed envelope to
ELLIOT RIGHT WAY BOOKS, BRIGHTON ROAD,
LOWER KINGSWOOD, TADWORTH, SURREY, KT20 6TD,U.K.
or visit our web site at www.right-way.co.uk